NO FRILLS Exam Prep Books

Intellectual Properties, Trademarks and Copyrights

ExamREVIEW.NET (a.k.a. ExamREVIEW) is an independent content developer not associated/affiliated with the certification vendor(s) mentioned throughout this book. The name(s), title(s) and award(s) of the certification exam(s) mentioned in this book are the trademark(s) of the respective certification vendor(s). We mention these name(s) and/or the relevant terminologies only for describing the relevant exam process(es) and knowledge.

ExamREVIEW(TM) and ExamFOCUS(TM) are our own trademarks for publishing and marketing self-developed examprep books worldwide. The EXAMREVIEW.NET web site has been created on the Internet since January 2001. The EXAMFOCUS.NET division has its web presence established since 2009.

Contents of this book are fully copyrighted. We develop study material entirely on our own. Braindump is strictly prohibited. We provide essential knowledge contents, NOT any generalized "study system" kind of "pick-the-right-answer-every time" techniques or "visit this link" referrals.

Contents Update

All books come with LIFE TIME FREE UPDATES. When you find a newer version of the purchased book all you need to do is to go and download. **Please check our web site's Free Updates section regularly:**

http://www.examreview.net/free_updates.htm

Page Formatting and Typeface

To accommodate the needs of those with weaker vision, we use LARGER PRINT throughout the book whenever practical. The text in this book was created using Garamond (size 16). A little bit of page resizing, however, may have happened along the actual book printing process.

The Exam

The Microsoft Technology Associate MTA certification is an entry-level certification which serves as a good starting point for students and educators who may eventually progress to the higher programs. Simply put, it assesses the foundational knowledge necessary to pursue MCSE, MCSD and the like.

The MTA certification focuses more on knowledge and a little less on skills. However, the knowledge areas are all based on MS products so you must know those products inside and out. Questions on the general knowledge are relatively easy. Product and technology specific technical questions, however, are way more difficult. This is why we developed this study product - we focus on those difficult topics that involve difficult technical skills. We want you to be able to answer these difficult questions and secure exam success accordingly. Exam 98-364: Database Fundamentals is designed to allow candidates to assess their knowledge of and skills with SQL Server databases and operations. Topics covered include:

- Understanding Core Database Concepts

- Creating Database Objects

- Manipulating Data

- Understanding Data Storage

- Administering a Database

This ExamFOCUS book focuses on the more difficult topics that will likely make a difference in exam results. The book is NOT intended to guide you through every single official topic. You should therefore use this book together with other reference books for the best possible preparation outcome. **You should download the evaluation copy of SQL Server and play with it. Download the ISO image file and burn a DVD disc out of it, then perform installation accordingly.** Officially the exam covers SQL Server 2008. However, the topics covered can apply to SQL Server 2012 as well. Therefore, you may use either version for practice purpose.

Table of Contents (MTA SQL Exam)

Server Management and Administration

Overview

A server can have multiple instances of SQL Server installed and running, and that each of these instances can contain one or more databases. In a database the object ownership groups are known as schemas. Each schema has multiple database objects including tables, views, and stored procedures. All these databases are stored in the file system in files, and that these files are often grouped into filegroups.

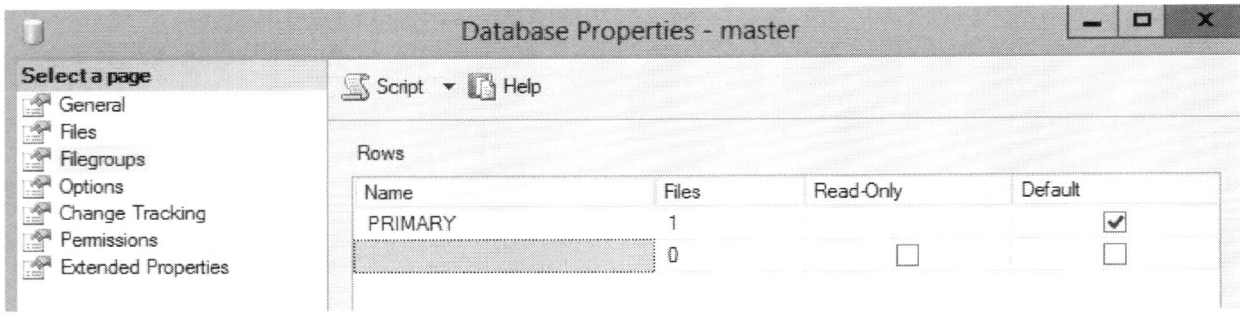

Management Studio and other Configuration Tools

You use the SQL Server Configuration Manager to manage the various SQL Server services. You also use it to setup the SQL clients/client protocols. Note that the default client TCP port is 1433.

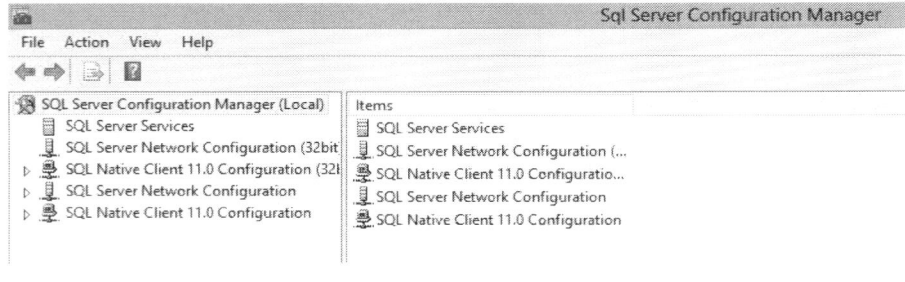

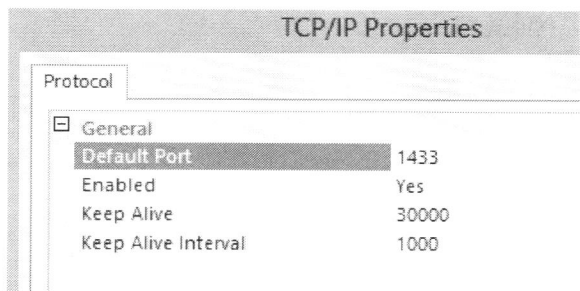

You use the Reporting Services Configuration Manager to configure and manage the reporting services.

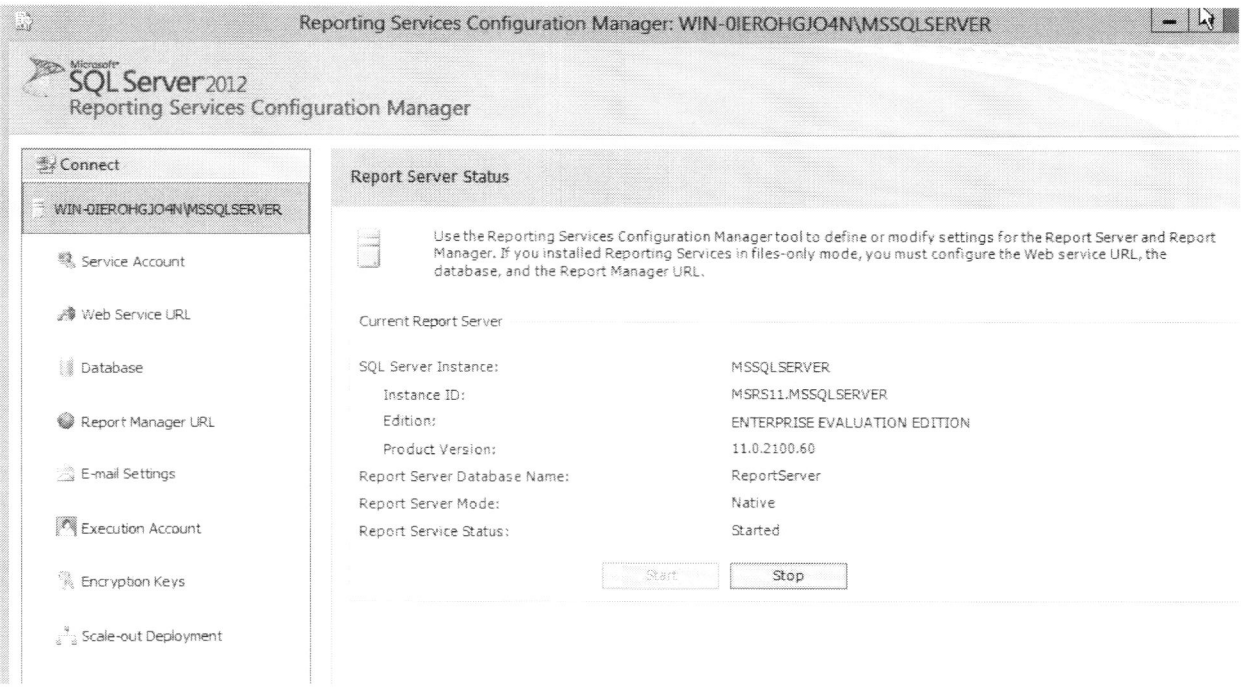

SQL Server can capture events in the Database Engine as they occur. The captured events become event class instances that you can monitor in the trace process. You rely on the SQL Server Profiler to utilize traces. Trace files are using the .trc extension. With SQL Server Profiler you can capture and save data about an event to a file or a table so that you can analyze later. You can even create templates that define the event classes and data columns to be included in the various traces. There are some predefined templates you can use as well.

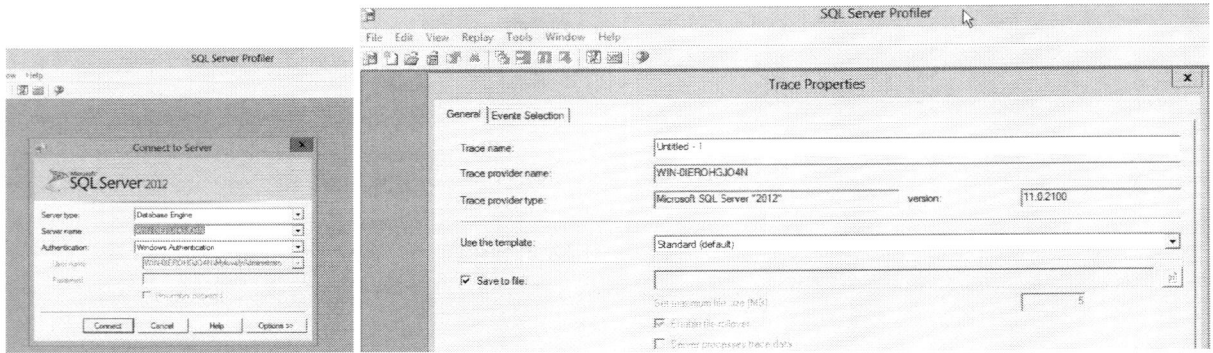

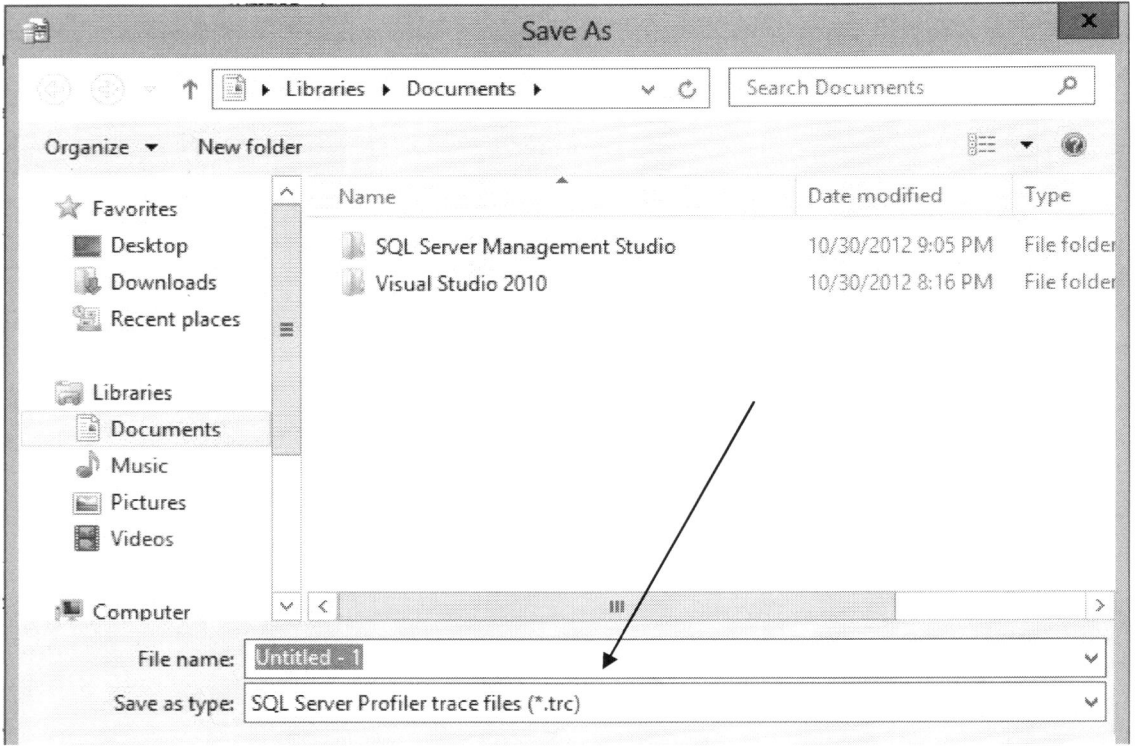

The Standard template can capture all the stored procedures and T-SQL batches that are run. You can use it to monitor the general database server activities. TSQL is a template that captures all T-SQL statements submitted to SQL Server by clients and the time issued. You use it for debugging client applications. TSQL_Duration can capture statements submitted and their execution time. You use them to identify the slower queries. TSQL_Grouped is a template that captures all statements submitted, with information grouped by clients that submitted the statement. You use it to investigate queries from certain client. TSQL_SPs is a template that captures detailed information about the executing stored procedures. SQL Server Profiler uses the Standard template as the default one but you can always switch to another one as you see fit.

The Management Studio is the primary interface for managing the databases.

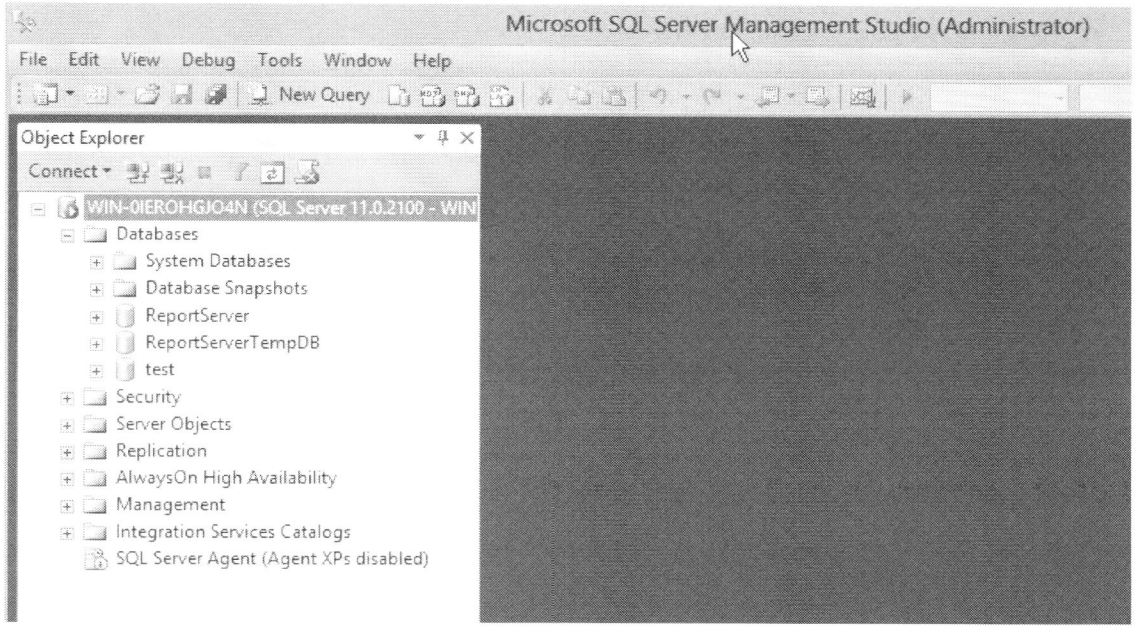

From there you can view the properties of the databases created. On the left pane there is the Object Explorer. You right click on an object to access the object's properties. Server role and security settings are all accessible from there.

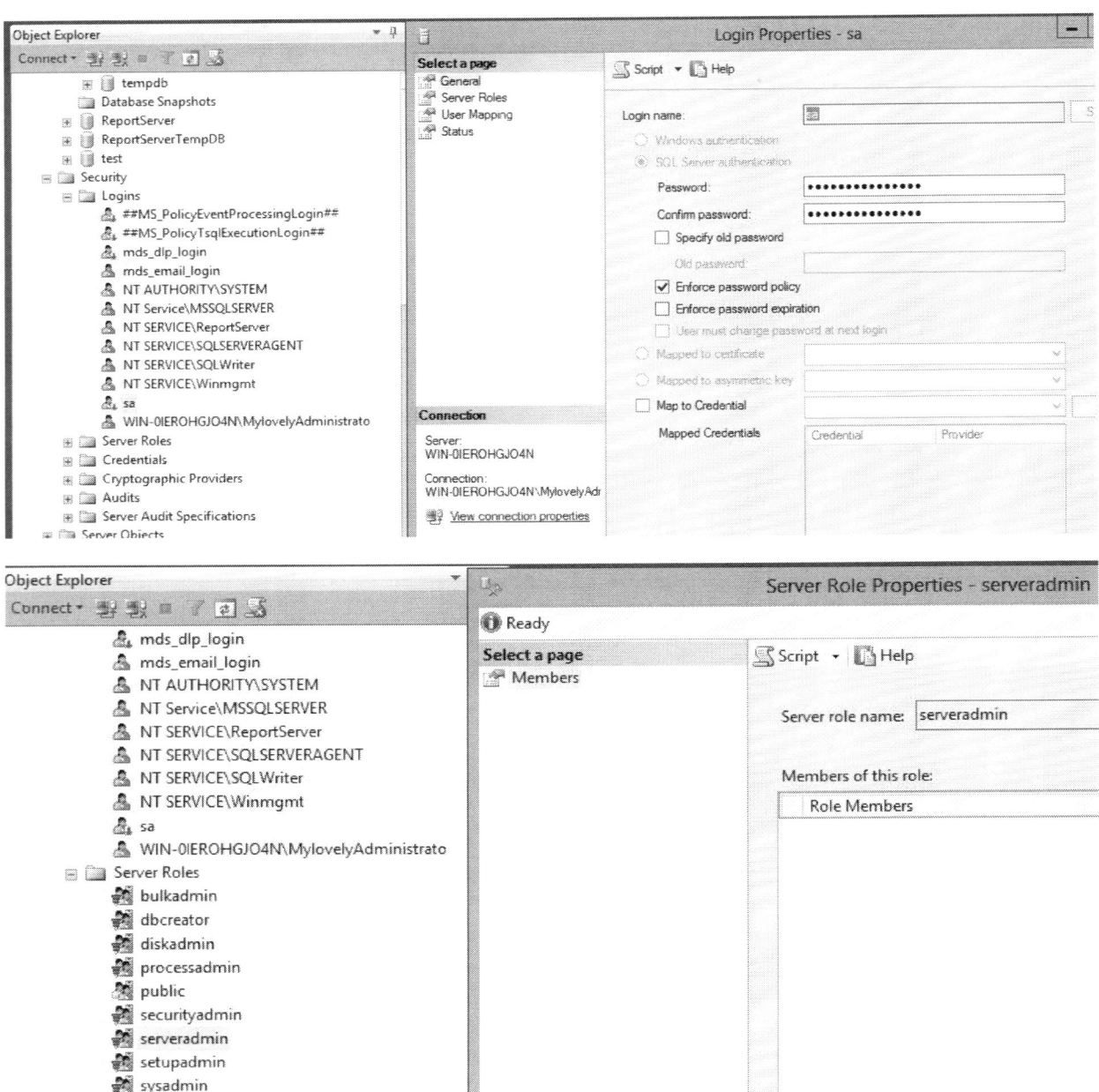

The Query Windows provides a basic editor you can use to write T-SQL statements and scripts. However, even a regular text editor can do the job.

```
SQLQuery1.sql - WI...yAdministrato (56))  ×
    USE [master]
    GO

 /* For security reasons the login is created
 /****** Object:  Login [sa]     Script Date: 1
    CREATE LOGIN [sa] WITH PASSWORD=N'w{Òp:?Q/Ú*ßh
    GO

    ALTER LOGIN [sa] DISABLE
    GO

    ALTER SERVER ROLE [sysadmin] ADD MEMBER [sa]
    GO
```

Server Level Roles

SQL Server by default offers 9 fixed server roles, and that those permissions granted to these roles cannot be altered. You may, however, create user-defined server roles and add server-level permissions to your very own user-defined server roles.

● With the sysadmin fixed server role one can perform any activity in the server.

● With the serveradmin fixed server role one can change server-wide configuration options and even shut down the server.

● With the securityadmin fixed server role one can manage logins and their properties. They can also GRANT, DENY, and REVOKE permissions at server-level and also database-level permissions (assuming they have access to the database). They may also reset passwords for all SQL Server logins.

● With the processadmin fixed server role one can end processes that are running.

- With the setupadmin fixed server role one may add and remove linked servers at wish.

- With the bulkadmin fixed server role can execute the BULK INSERT statement.

- With the diskadmin fixed server role one can manage disk files.

- With the dbcreator fixed server role one can create, alter, drop, and restore any database but may not alter databases of the others.

In fact, every SQL Server login belongs to the public server role. When a server principal does not have any specific permission on an object the user will inherit the permissions granted to public.

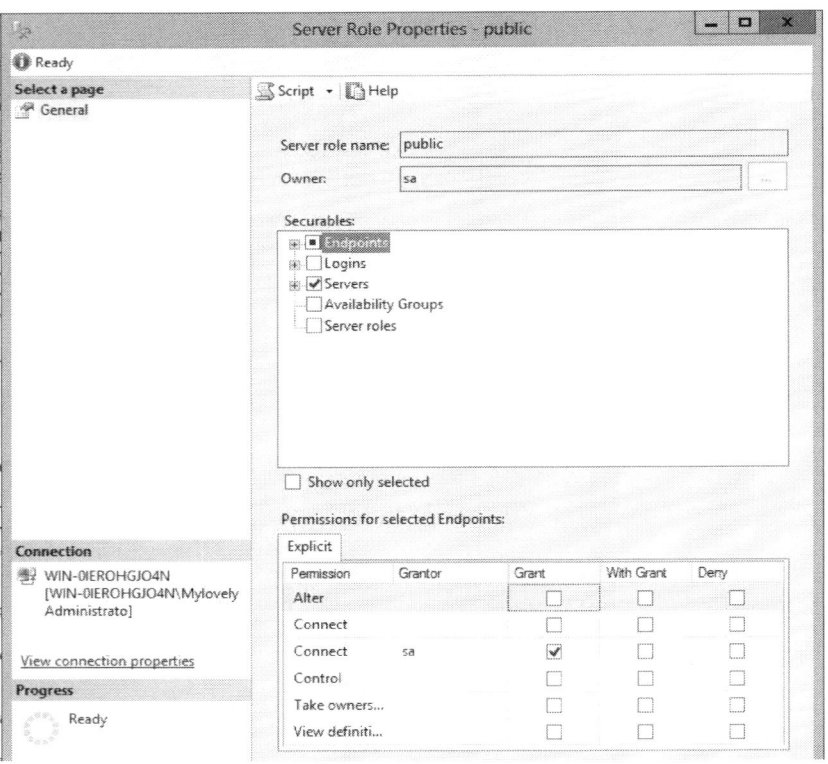

Logins and Credentials

You can configure logins and their passwords from the Management Studio.

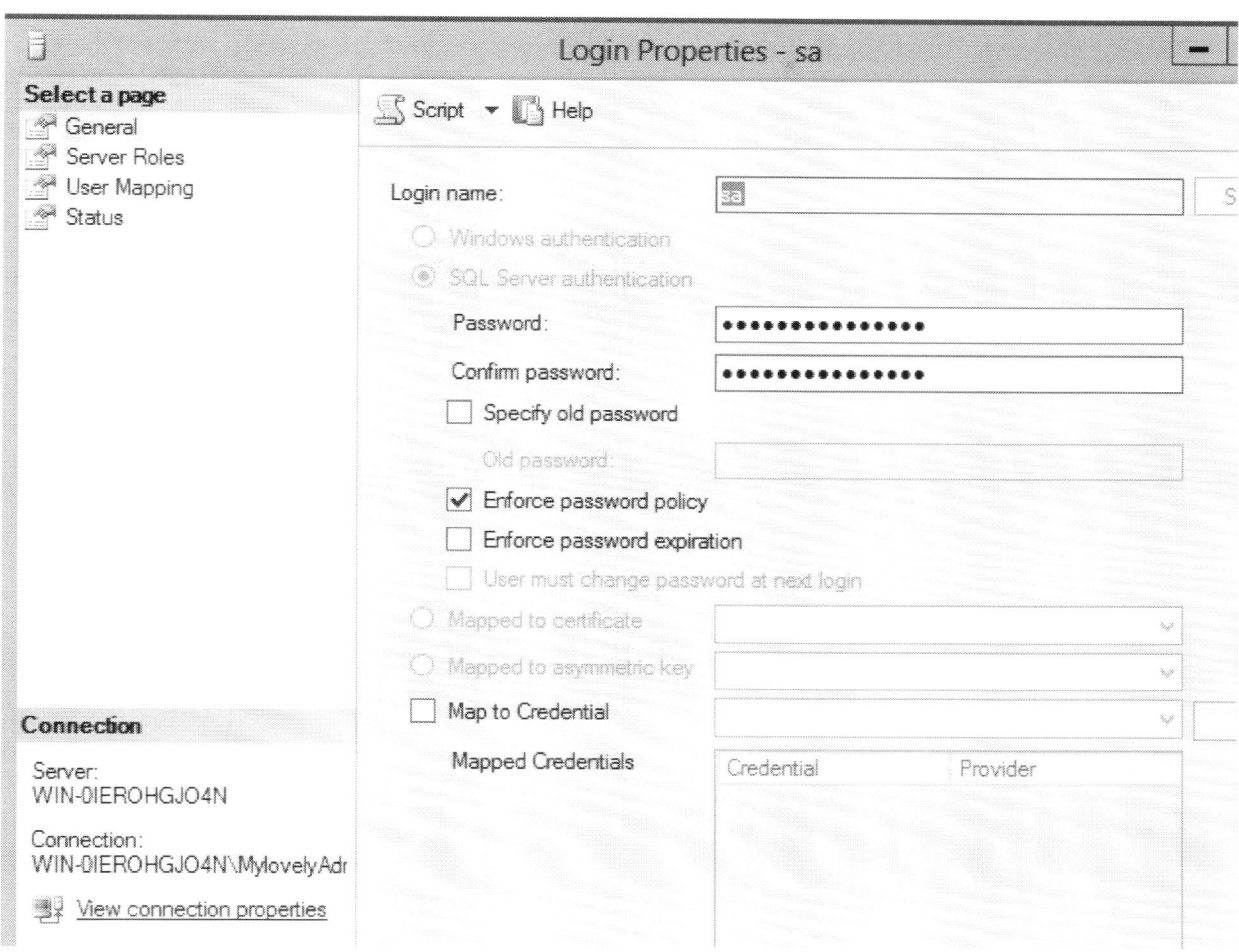

An alternative is to use CREATE LOGIN. There are some options that can be used with it. HASHED is an option that specifies that the password placed after the PASSWORD argument is already hashed. You should use it only when migrating databases from one server to another. You should NOT use it to create new logins. With MUST_CHANGE, SQL Server will prompt the user for a new password the first time he uses his new login. CHECK_EXPIRATION tells whether password expiration policy should be enforced on this particular login. The default for it is OFF.

CHECK_POLICY says that the Windows password policies of the local server computer should be enforced on this particular login. The default for it is ON. If your Windows policy requires strong passwords, passwords must be complex. WINDOWS is for specifying that the login is to be mapped to a Windows login.

Credentials allow SQL Server Authentication users to possess an identity outside of SQL Server. A credential can be mapped to more than SQL Server logins. HOWEVER, a SQL Server login can only be mapped to a single credential. Also, a credential cannot be mapped to the sa account. You may use CREATE CREDENTIAL or the Management Studio to create credentials.

It is possible to script the logins using the Script Login as option. You can call up the Query Editor from there and write scripts.

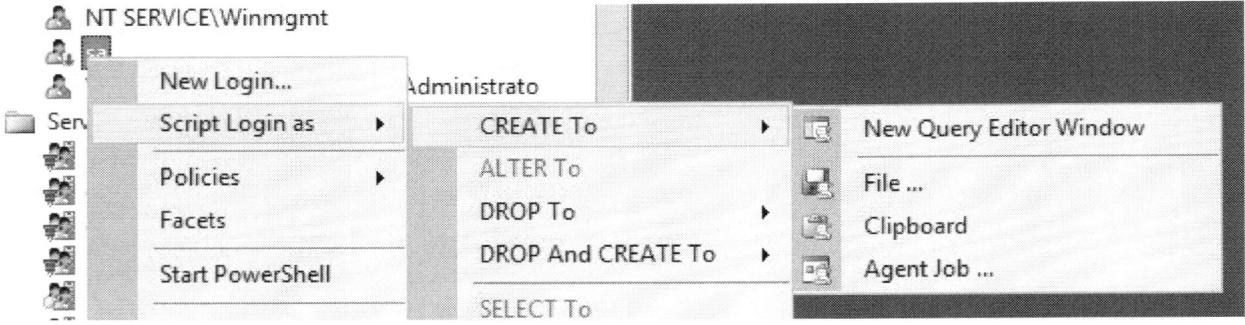

One popular use of scripting here is to transfer logins to a new version of SQL server. MS KB 246133 has some pretty good examples.

You want to know that there are optional password policies available for SQL Server logins, which are:

- User must change password at next login

- Enforce password expiration

- Enforce password policy

Additionally, the Windows password policies of the server computer are also enforced for SQL Server logins. SQL Server Authentication is a good choice if you need to provide support for older applications or third party applications, or that your environment has mixed operating systems in place where users are authenticated not only by a Windows domain. Even if Windows is the only OS, you want to allow users to connect from unknown or even untrusted domains. And keep in mind, Web-based applications which have their users creating their own identities will not be able to authenticate through Windows. Simply put, compatibility is the biggest advantage offered by SQL Server authentication.

Logon Triggers

Logon triggers are triggers that can fire stored procedures when a LOGON event is raised (which is when a user session is established with an instance). Do note that logon triggers fire only after authentication is finished and before the user session is actually established. They will not fire when authentication fails. It is often a good idea to use logon triggers to audit and control server sessions. You can create them via CREATE TRIGGER.

There can be multiple triggers defined on the LOGON event. These triggers differ from event notifications in that they are raised synchronously with events, whereas event notifications are not synchronous.

The Database Engine

Database Engine service is the executable process of the SQL Server Database Engine. SQL Server Agent service is a Windows service that executes scheduled administrative tasks. SQL Server Browser service is a Windows service that listens for incoming requests. Note that a single instance of this Browser service can be used for all instances of SQL Server installed on the same server computer. If you pause the Database Engine service, you will prevent new users from connecting to the Database Engine but those users who are already connected can still work without termination. The SQL Server Agent service, on the other hand, simply cannot be paused.

There are other options. -c means shortening the startup time when starting SQL Server from the command prompt. -f means starting an instance with minimal configuration, which is very useful if the setting of a particular configuration value is preventing the server from starting. -g can be used to specify the size of memory that SQL Server can leave available for allocations within the SQL Server process outside the SQL Server memory pool. -m "Client Application Name" can limit connections to a specified client application. -n disallows the use of Windows application log to record SQL Server events. -s allows you to start only a named instance of SQL Server. -E can increase the number of extents allocated for each file in a filegroup.

Transaction Modes

Autocommit mode is the transaction management mode in use by default. What it means is that every T-SQL statement will be committed or rolled back when it is completed. If a statement completes without problems, it will be committed. If it has errors, it will get rolled back. In fact this mode is also the default for ADO, OLE DB, ODBC, and DB-Library.

If there is a BEGIN TRANSACTION statement, an explicit transaction will start so autocommit will end. If SET IMPLICIT_TRANSACTIONS is in effect, the connection will change to implicit transaction mode, which will also end the autocommit transaction mode. Normally, the implicit transaction mode will stay in effect until the connection executes a SET IMPLICIT_TRANSACTIONS OFF statement. Practically, the COMMIT TRANSACTION statement when execute will mark the end of a successful implicit or explicit transaction. On the other hand, ROLLBACK TRANSACTION will roll back an explicit or implicit transaction to the beginning of the transaction and remove all data modifications made.

When a connection is run under the implicit transaction mode, the instance will automatically start a new transaction after the current transaction is either committed or rolled back. You do not need to write any statement to mark the start of a new transaction.

Resource Governor

Resource Governor is a feature you can use to specify limits (even in real time) on resource consumption by incoming requests. To enable Resource Governor via Object Explorer, you expand the Management node until you find Resource Governor. Right click on it and then click Enable. Or, to configure its properties, click Properties to open the Resource Governor Properties page. You may also enable it via ALTER RESOURCE GOVERNOR RECONFIGURE.

A workload group serves as nothing more than a container for session requests with similar or identical classification criteria. You use it for aggregate monitoring of sessions. In Object Explorer, you can expand the Management node until you find the resource pool that contains the workload group to be modified. You then right click the Workload Groups folder and choose New Workload Group. To do it via T-SQL, first run CREATE WORKLOAD GROUP to specify the property values, then run ALTER RESOURCE GOVERNOR RECONFIGURE.

When configuring the Resource Governor properties you can configure the resource pool as well. Do note that the max CPU percentage must NOT be lower than the minimum CPU percentage. Also, the max memory percentage must not be lower than the minimum memory percentage. And the sums of the minimum CPU percentages and minimum memory percentages for all of the available resource pools must not go over 100. In fact you can use CREATE RESOURCE POOL and then ALTER RESOURCE GOVERNOR RECONFIGURE to achieve the same.

Finally, you may choose to configure Resource Governor via a template in SQL Server Management Studio. To do so, from SQL Server Management

Studio you go to View - Template Explorer. Expand Resource Governor and then double click on Configure Resource Governor.

Locks and Latches

Locks are always held on SQL Server resources during a transaction for preventing concurrent use of resources by multiple different transactions. When a lock is held on a row by a transaction, no other transaction can modify that row until the lock gets released. When you minimize locks you increase concurrency and improve performance. Latches are internal SQL Server resource locks related to user activity and resource usage. It has a lot to do with performance bottlenecks.

Transaction Isolation Levels

The relevant command is SET TRANSACTION ISOLATION LEVEL. Transaction isolation levels define the type of locks that can be acquired on read operations. Only one isolation level option can be set at a time, and that it will remain set for that connection.

Transactions running with READ UNCOMMITTED would not issue shared locks to prevent other transactions from modifying data read by the current transaction. READ UNCOMMITTED transactions are not blocked by exclusive locks as well. Reading uncommitted modifications means dirty reads. With this allowed you are just like setting NOLOCK on all tables in all SELECT statements that take place in a transaction. READ COMMITTED is more restrictive, as it means that statements cannot read data that has been changed but not yet committed by other transactions. This effectively disallows dirty reads and is the SQL Server default setting. Note that when READ_COMMITTED_SNAPSHOT is OFF (which is the default), the Database Engine will use shared locks to prevent other transactions from modifying rows when the current transaction is reading them.

REPEATABLE READ means statements cannot read data modified but not yet committed by other transactions. At the same time, no other transactions can modify data that has been read by the current transaction, at least not until the current transaction is fully completed. Shared locks are imposed on all data read by each statement in the transaction. They remain until the transaction is completed. SNAPSHOT means a transaction can only recognize data modifications committed prior to the start of the transaction. Data modifications made by others after the start of the current transaction will simply be invisible.

When you select, modify or insert rows, you can use table hints to apply locks. ROWLOCK specifies that row locks are to be taken. TABLOCK means the acquired lock is to be applied at the table level. TABLOCKX refers to an exclusive lock on the table. UPDLOCK are update locks that are to be held until a transaction is completed. XLOCK can be specified with ROWLOCK, PAGLOCK, or TABLOCK for applying exclusive locks. SERIALIZABLE produces the same effect as setting HOLDLOCK on all tables in all SELECT statements within a transaction.

You can query sys.dm_tran_locks to find out if there are many locks outstanding.

SQL Server Agent

SQL Server Agent is the feature for database automation. It is a feature designed for processing alerts and running scheduled jobs. When alerts are triggered and when scheduled jobs are run, you can notify SQL Server operators through the SQL Server Agent, which can send out the relevant alerts and notifications through email via Database Mail or the deprecated SQL Mail. To use the former, you need to configure one or more databases as mail hosts. You also need to define client settings so that the SQL Server Agent can send out email messages via a SMTP mail server.

To instruct SQL Server Agent to execute a job immediately, use sp_start_job. Or, you can use sp_update_job to make changes to a job. You can also use sp_get_schedule_description to extract and read the job schedule, or query sysjobs_view to find out further information on the various jobs. sp_help_jobactivity can produce information on the status of a job run, while sp_help_jobcount can produce a count on how many jobs a schedule is tied to.

sp_configure

You may use sp_configure to show or change server-level settings. However, it is not for changing database-level settings. Database level settings can be changed via ALTER DATABASE. To make changes related to only the current user session, use the SET statement instead. Some configuration options require a server stop and restart. To update the currently configured value of a configuration option that has been changed with sp_configure, use RECONFIGURE. Why would you use sp_configure instead of the management studio GUI? While the most commonly used server configuration options are available through the GUI, ALL configuration options are accessible through this sp_configure stored procedure!

Affinity Mask Options

Windows Server allows one to assign processors to specific threads. SQL Server supports this kind of processor affinity with two affinity mask options, which are affinity mask and affinity I/O mask. The former can be used to dynamically control CPU affinity. It can be configured without requiring a restart of the instance via sp_configure with either RECONFIGURE or RECONFIGURE WITH OVERRIDE. SQL Server will enable a new CPU scheduler which replaces the existing CPU scheduler. I/O affinity tasks, on the other hand, can directly affect the I/O affinity mask. In any case the RECONFIGURE command can verify that the normal CPU and I/O affinities are mutually exclusive.

Since SQL Server 2012, ALTER SERVER CONFIGURATION can be used with the PROCESS AFFINITY argument for configuring processor affinity options.

Memory Options

Generally you should allow SQL Server to adjust and use memory dynamically. If you really want to set the memory options manually, use the Management Studio GUI or sp_configure. You may want to make such settings by hand if there are multiple different applications running together -

you may want to set the min server memory and the max server memory to span a range of memory values. You set the min server memory value to guarantee a minimum amount of memory available to an instance (in reality the guarantee is never absolute). On the other hand, you use max server memory to establish maximum memory usage settings for each instance.

Questions:

1. What can be done with SQL Server Profiler?

2. Describe the TSQL template.

3. Describe the TSQL_Duration template.

4. Describe the TSQL_Grouped template.

5. Describe the sysadmin fixed server role.

6. Describe the serveradmin fixed server role.

7. With CREATE LOGIN, what is the HASHED option for?

8. With CREATE LOGIN, what is the MUST_CHANGE option for?

9. What are credentials?

10. Logon triggers are triggers that can fire stored procedures when a _____ event is raised.

11. Describe the autocommit mode.

12. Transaction isolation levels define:

13. What is a workload group?

14. What is REPEATABLE READ?

15. What is SNAPSHOT in the context of transaction?

16. You can query _____ to find out if there are many locks outstanding.

17. SQL Server Agent is the feature for:

18. You may use what stored procedure to show or change server-level settings?

19. Database level settings can be changed via what statement?

20. What stored procedure can you use to instruct SQL Server Agent to execute a job immediately?

21. What stored procedure can you use to make changes to a job?

22. What stored procedure can you use to extract and read the job schedules?

23. How do you setup Database Mail?

24. What is the biggest advantage offered by SQL Server authentication?

25. When you minimize locks you can:

26. What are latches?

Answers:

1. *With SQL Server Profiler you can capture and save data about an event to a file or a table so that you can analyze later. You can even create templates that define the event classes and data columns to be included in the various traces.*

2. *TSQL is a template that captures all T-SQL statements submitted to SQL Server by clients and the time issued. You use it for debugging client applications.*

3. *TSQL_Duration can capture statements submitted and their execution time. You use them to identify the slower queries.*

4. *TSQL_Grouped is a template that captures all statements submitted, with information grouped by clients that submitted the statement.*

5. *With the sysadmin fixed server role one can perform any activity in the server.*

6. *With the serveradmin fixed server role one can change server-wide configuration options and even shut down the server.*

7. *With CREATE LOGIN, HASHED is an option that specifies that the password placed after the PASSWORD argument is already hashed.*

8. *With CREATE LOGIN's MUST_CHANGE option, SQL Server will prompt the user for a new password the first time he uses his new login.*

9. *Credentials allow SQL Server Authentication users to possess an identity outside of SQL Server. A credential can be mapped to more than SQL Server logins.*

10. *Logon triggers are triggers that can fire stored procedures when a LOGON event is raised (which is when a user session is established with an instance).*

11. *Autocommit mode is the transaction management mode in use by default. What it means is that every T-SQL statement will be committed or rolled back when it is completed.*

12. *Transaction isolation levels define the type of locks that can be acquired on read operations. Only one isolation level option can be set at a time, and that it will remain set for that connection.*

13. *A workload group serves as nothing more than a container for session requests with similar or identical classification criteria. You use it for aggregate monitoring of sessions.*

14. *REPEATABLE READ means statements cannot read data modified but not yet committed by other transactions. At the same time, no other transactions can modify*

data that has been read by the current transaction, at least not until the current transaction is fully completed.

15. SNAPSHOT means a transaction can only recognize data modifications committed prior to the start of the transaction. Data modifications made by others after the start of the current transaction will simply be invisible.

16. You can query sys.dm_tran_locks to find out if there are many locks outstanding

17. SQL Server Agent is the feature for database automation. It is a feature designed for processing alerts and running scheduled jobs.

18. You may use sp_configure to show or change server-level settings. However, it is not for changing database-level settings.

19. Database level settings can be changed via ALTER DATABASE.

20. To instruct SQL Server Agent to execute a job immediately, use sp_start_job.

21. You can use sp_update_job to make changes to a job.

22. You can use sp_get_schedule_description to extract and read the job schedule.

23. To use Database Mail, you should configure msdb as the database mail host, then designate a profile for it and grant profile access to the SQL Server Agent service account.

24. Compatibility is the biggest advantage offered by SQL Server authentication.

25. When you minimize locks you increase concurrency and improve performance.

26. Latches are internal SQL Server resource locks related to user activity and resource usage.

Database Design, Management and Administration

Logical & Physical Design

Physical design refers to the process of producing a detailed database specific data model to meet end user requirements. Conceptual database design is all about constructing a data model for dealing with a real world issue without giving any physical considerations. ER Modeling involves developing a visual representation of the real world problem as an ERD Entity Relationship Diagram and have the details modeled in terms of entities, attributes and relations. Logical database design which is not specific to the database requires the construction of a model of information that can be mapped into the various SQL Server database objects. Data cardinality refers to the uniqueness of data values contained in a column. With high data cardinality the values of a data column are very uncommon, that uniqueness is more likely. With normal data cardinality the data values are uncommon and never unique. With low data cardinality there are very limited values, such as Yes/No, True/False…etc.

Normalizing a database is a process that involves deploying methods to separate data into multiple related tables. With a greater number of smaller tables that have fewer columns, you get a normalized database which is good for OLTP that requires fast write and fast update. With a few large tables that have more columns per table you get a de-normalized database that is good for OLAP as OLAP requires fast read and computation on the fly. OLTP stands for Online Transaction Processing, which is optimized for handling transactions. OLAP stands for Online Analytical Processing, which is optimized for adhoc result aggregation and summarization of large amount of data.

First normal form 1NF requires that you eliminate duplicative columns from the same table and create separate tables for each group of related data. You also need to identify each row with a unique column or a unique set of columns to serve as the primary key. Second Normal Form 2NF further requires that you remove all subsets of data that apply to multiple rows of a table and relocate them in other separate tables. You also need to create relationships between these new tables using foreign keys. Third Normal Form 3NF further requires that you remove all those columns that are not dependent on the primary key. Fourth Normal Form 4NF further requires that all multi-valued dependencies be removed. Denormalization requires data redundancy but can reduce the number of joins to be used during query.

Partitioning a table means breaking it into multiple smaller ones. With horizontal partitioning you partition the table by grouping the rows based on a particular criteria such as an ID range. With vertical partitioning you have a table portioned based on the frequency of access of the columns - you split the table into multiple smaller tables where each table holds only a few columns. You may also partition the indexed columns and non-indexed columns into separate tables, or split LOB and VARCHARMAX columns into separate tables.

Performance Tuning

The performance of SQL Server can be affected due to these factors:

- Hardware

- Network infrastructure

- OS configuration

- Server side applications

- Client side applications

It is recommended that you use baseline measurements to measure the peak and off-peak hours of operation; the production-query or batch-command response times; as well as the database backup and restore completion times. You should then determine if performance improvements can be made. You also want to determine user activity so to find out the types of query your users are issuing as well as who is connecting to your SQL Server. You may then troubleshoot the problems and test the applications accordingly. In particular there is the Database Engine Tuning Advisor DTA which can examine how queries are processed and then recommends how you may improve the query processing performance. This tool basically replaces the Index Tuning Wizard found in the earlier SQL Server releases. You may use its GUI or the command prompt utility known as dta.

You may also want to monitor individual user activities so to identify the kinds of blocking transactions or slowed performance. You want to know the types of transactions run, the number of inefficient ad hoc queries found, and the types of transactions that require the most resources. Active User Tasks displays information for those active user connections made to the server. Resource Waits tells the wait state information. Data File I/O reveals /O information for the database data and log files. Recent Expensive Queries identifies those most expensive queries. You may open the Activity Monitor GUI via SQL Server Management Studio's Object Explorer. Since it monitors activities in real time, you want to set the refresh interval to no less than 10 seconds or server performance can be affected.

The System Databases

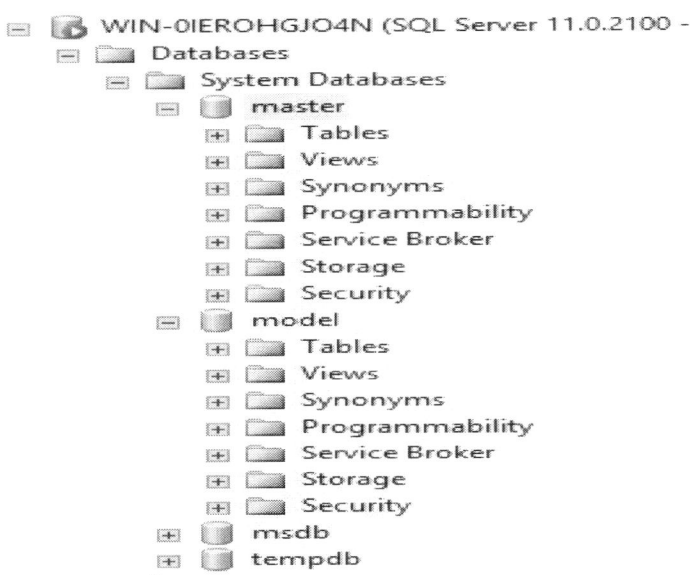

The master database is for recording system-level information for an instance. The msdb database is for used by the SQL Server Agent to schedule alerts and jobs. The model database is the template for all databases created on the instance. The tempdb database is simply a workspace for holding temporary objects and result sets. The resource database is read-only and is for holding system objects that are included with SQL Server. These system objects are physically persisted inside the resource database although they show up in the sys schema of every database (which is a logical representation). **You should have the master database backed up whenever a user database is created, changed, or dropped.**

Generally you should not directly update information in the system objects. Instead you should use administration utilities such as SQL Server Management Studio or T-SQL scripts and stored procedures. You should also not query these objects directly. Instead you can do so through the various system catalog views, through the Windows Management Instrumentation interface, or through the various T-SQL stored procedures and built-in functions.

Catalog views are designed for returning information used by the SQL Server Database Engine. Do note that some catalog views simply inherit rows from other catalog views. These are the views related to databases and files:

- sys.backup_devices

- sys.database_files

- sys.database_mirroring

- sys.database_recovery_status

- sys.databases

- sys.master_files

You should back up the master database using a regular backup schedule plus additional backup after any substantial update.

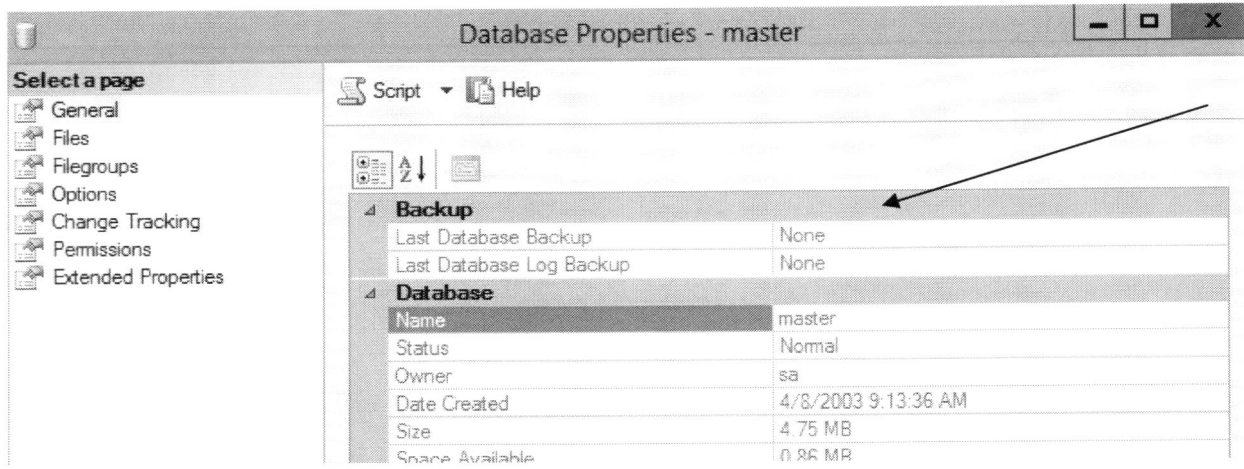

On the other hand, you should create only full database backups of the model database as required since it rarely changes. msdb should be backed up whenever it is updated. Both the resource database and the tempdb cannot be backed up. As a side note you can perform a file-based or a disk-based backup on the mssqlsystemresource.mdf file which holds the resource database. You simply cannot back it up using SQL Server backup. Note that the system databases can only be restored from backups created on the version of SQL Server that the server instance is currently running. To restore, the instance must be running and that the master database must be accessible and partly or fully usable.

In order to move a system database data or log file in a planned manner, you need to first run ALTER DATABASE database_name MODIFY FILE (NAME = logical_name , FILENAME = 'new_path\os_file_name'). Then you stop the instance and shut down the server if needed. Move the file, and then restart the instance.

Files and Filegroups

SQL Server's Filegroups feature uses a proportional fill mechanism across all the files within each filegroup. When all the files in a filegroup are full, the Database Engine will automatically expand one file at a time. Generally, using files and filegroups can improve database performance since a database can be created across multiple disks, and that a table can be created in a pre-specified filegroup. In fact, databases that is made of multiple filegroups can be backed up and restored in stages or individually - so you have better flexibility. Do keep in mind, a file can only be a member of one single filegroup, and that transaction log files can never join any filegroups. A file or filegroup can be used only by one single database.

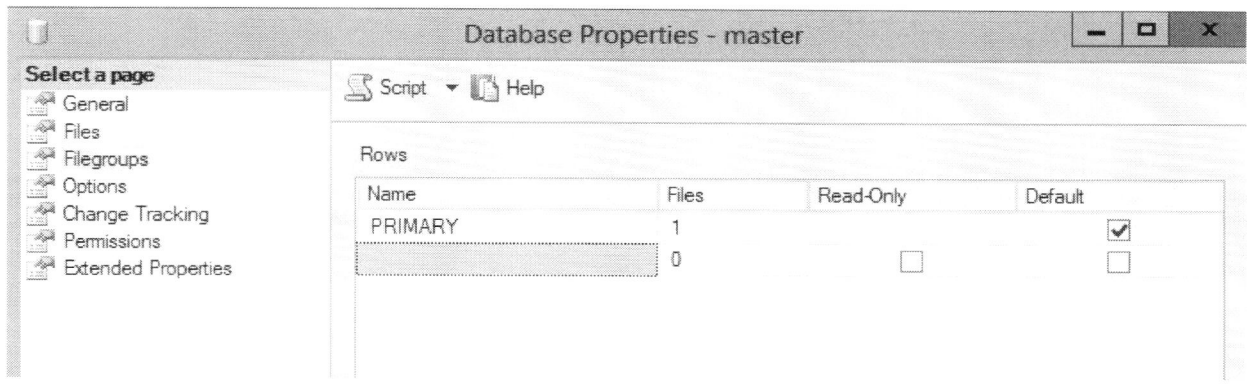

When you use CREATE DATABASE, there are several relevant options. FILENAME lets you specify the physical filename. SIZE and MAXSIZE are pretty much self explanatory. When size is not supplied, the size of the primary file in the model database will be used for the primary file. When a secondary data file or log file is created with no size specified, the default will be 1 MB. Do realize that the size you specify for the primary file must be at least as large as the primary file in the model database. UNLIMITED means the file can grow until the disk is full. Still, if it is a log file there is still a size limit of 2TB. If it is a data file the max is 16 TB.

When a new database is created, the primary file group is created with the primary data file is included in the primary file group. It serves as the default group. To make use of a secondary data file you need to first create a new file group and mark that file group as Default, then create a new data file in .ndf format and set it to become part of the new file group. Tables and indexes should be in separate file groups. Logs should be on another disk. Proper sizing of database objects is important since "Auto grow" and "Auto shrink" are costly processes and should be avoided as much as possible.

Regarding the ALTER DATABASE statement, these are the relevant options:

ADD FILE

... TO FILEGROUP

REMOVE FILE

MODIFY FILE

ADD FILEGROUP

REMOVE FILEGROUP

MODIFY FILEGROUP

Keep in mind, you may not add or remove files when BACKUP is running. You can have max 32,767 files and 32,767 filegroups for each database. The primary file group should be used to only keep system objects. It should not be used as the default file group. User objects should be placed somewhere else. If you have physical disk drives you should create multiple physical files per file group and if possible host one file per disk to spread out the I/O. A separate file group should be created for indexes. Text and image columns should be placed in a different file group on a different physical disk since they are I/O heavy. The log file must be placed on a different physical drive since logging is for sure very write intensive!

Single User Mode

If you choose to set the database to single user mode, note that other users connected to the database will be cut off without warning. The database will remain in single-user mode even if you log off. At that point, a different single user can connect to the database. Before setting the database to SINGLE_USER, you must ensure that the AUTO_UPDATE_STATISTICS_ASYNC option is OFF. To configure this, from the Management Studio GUI you look into Database Properties - Options - Restrict Access and select Single. To do so via T-SQL you use ALTER DATABASE with the SET SINGLE_USER option.

Temporary Tables

You can create temporary tables for complex operations. Local temporary tables are maintained only in the current session, while global temporary tables can survive across all the active sessions. The name specified for a temporary name should not exceed 116 characters, and you should prefix a global temporary table name with a double number sign ##, or a local temporary table with a single number sign #. When there are more than one temporary table created inside a stored procedure or batch, you must give them different names.

All temporary tables will be automatically dropped when the stored procedure is finished or explicitly dropped via DROP TABLE. Local temporary tables will always get dropped automatically at the end of their current sessions. A global temporary table will get automatically dropped when the session that created the table is completely ended.

Resizing a Database

You can adjust the database size via Object Explorer. Go into Database Properties - Files. To increase the size by enlarging an existing file you simply increase the value in the Initial Size column. To add a new file, click Add. You can also use ALTER DATABASE with the MODIFY FILE option to change file sizing.

Moving Databases

Generally, you can move system and user databases including data, log, and full-text catalog files by setting a new file location in the FILENAME clause of ALTER DATABASE. This is for moving within the same instance. To move to another instance, you need to first make the database offline. Do so via ALTER DATABASE with the SET OFFLINE option. Then move the files to the new location. For each file moved you set a new location using ALTER DATABASE with the option MODIFY FILE (NAME = logical_name, FILENAME = 'new location'). Finally, make it online again via ALTER DATABASE with the option SET ONLINE. If there is a server failure, before the move you must first stop the SQL Server service and then start it up again using NET START with the options /f /T3608. Only members of the sysadmin fixed role can move files under such circumstances.

Detach and Attach

The data and transaction log files of a database can be detached and attached to another instance of SQL Server so it will be easier to move the database. It works even across 32-bit and 64-bit environments. However, if you detach a read-only database you will lose information about the differential bases of your differential backups. Also, the system databases can never be attached.

You can use sp_detach_db to detach a database currently not in use from a server instance. You may optionally run UPDATE STATISTICS on all tables prior to detaching. If you need to move the detached database files, make sure you also move the log files even if you plan to create new log files.

To attach a database, you need to make sure all data files including those MDF and NDF files are available. You use CREATE DATABASE with the FOR ATTACH close. OR, you can attach or detach using the Management Studio GUI. From Object Explorer connect to the instance and expand it, then expand Databases and select the name of the user database you need to work with. Right click on it and point to Tasks.

Contained Databases

A contained database refers to a database isolated from other databases and also from the instance of SQL Server that hosts this database. A partially contained database is one that allows some but not all features that cross the database boundary. SQL Server 2012's contained database feature can support only a partially contained state. The types of users supported for contained databases include contained database users with passwords that are authenticated by the database, and authorized Windows users and members of authorized Windows groups who may connect directly to the database without logins in the master database. In any case, enabling partially contained databases means you delegate control over access to the instance to the owners of the database.

Backup and Recovery Models

A media set refers to an ordered collection of backup media, tapes or disk files. A media family includes those backups created on a single nonmirrored device or a set of mirrored devices within a media set. A backup set has the backup contents added to the media set via a successful backup process.

You use the BACKUP statement to make a full backup. OR, you connect to the instance in Object Explorer by clicking the server name and expanding the server tree. From there, expand Databases and select the target database to backup. Right click on it then point to Tasks and then click Back Up. This will call up the Back Up Database dialog box. On the other hand, to restore from a backup you point to Tasks - Restore and then click Database to open the Restore Database dialog box. The backup media can be a file (a local file or a remote file with a UNC name), a device (a logical backup device defined on the server instance) or a tape. Do realize that backups created by more recent version of SQL Server cannot be restored in any of the earlier versions. Also, as the database increases in size, full database backups can take a long time to finish.

To be practical, when dealing with a large database you should supplement a full database backup with a series of differential database backups. A differential backup simply captures the data that has changed since that full backup. Creating this kind of backups is way faster compared to creating a full backup since it records only the data that has changed since the full backup. It is especially useful when a subset of a database is modified relatively more often than the rest of the database. In any case, before you make a full backup you should first estimate the size required by using the sp_spaceused system stored procedure.

By default, backup compression is off. In fact, backup compression is a server-level configuration option. It is not always desirable since it is extremely processor hungry. Also, you cannot keep compressed and uncompressed backups in the same media set. Previous versions of SQL Server will also not be able to read the compressed backups.

The available recovery models are full, simple and bulk-logged recovery. They determine how much data loss is considered as acceptable after a failure and what types of recovery related functions are allowed. With the Simple model there is no log backup and that all log space will be reclaimed to keep space requirements small. It can only recover to the end of a backup. With the Full model log backups are required but there will be no work lost. It is also possible to restore to a specific point in time. Bulk logged also requires log backups. It permits high-performance bulk copy operations while cutting down log space. It is NOT possible to restore to a specific point in time though.

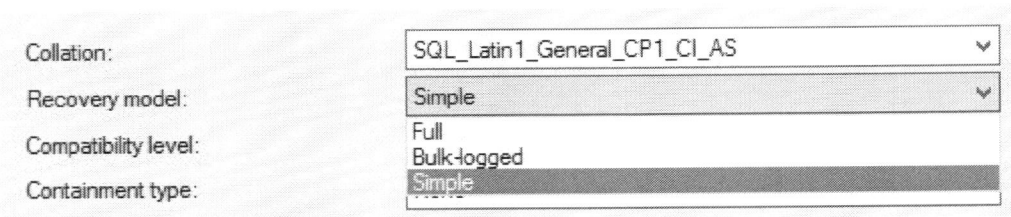

With a complete database restore, the whole database will be made offline for the duration of the restore, and that all data is recovered to a consistent point with no uncommitted transactions exist. This is called a simple recovery model - your database cannot be restored to a specific point in time.

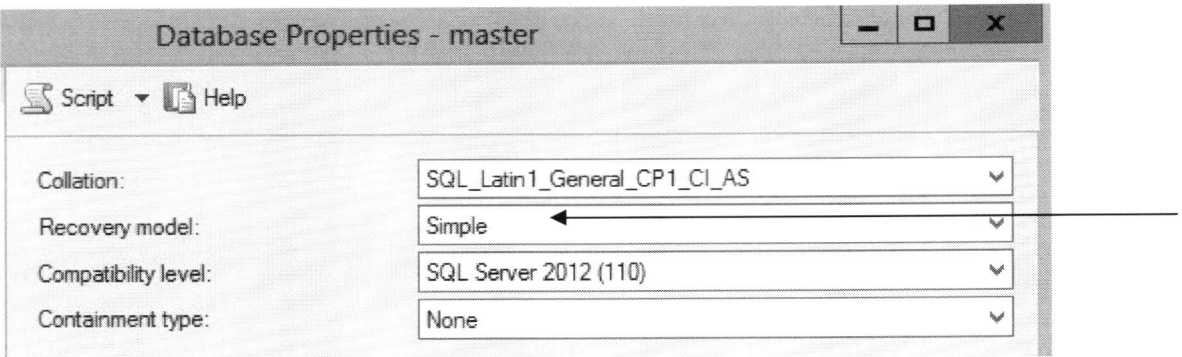

If your database uses the full or bulk-logged recovery model, you need to back up the transaction log regularly. A tail-log backup is special - it captures those log records that have not yet been backed up, which are usually located at the tail of the log, to prevent work loss. In fact, in order to recover a SQL Server database to its latest point in time, you need to back up the tail since the resulting tail-log backup will serve as the last backup of interest in the recovery effort.

When the transaction log is filled up, you need to back up the log and then free up disk space so that the log can automatically grow. You may also consider to move the log file to a disk drive with sufficient drive space, OR add a new log file on a different disk.

Maintenance Plan

In order to create or manage maintenance plans, you have to be a member of the sysadmin fixed server role. With a maintenance plan you can create an Integration Services package, which is to be run by a SQL Server Agent job manually or automatically at scheduled intervals. To create one you want to first expand the server where you want to create your management plan, assuming you are in Object Explorer. You then expand the Management folder, right click the Maintenance Plans folder and pick Maintenance Plan Wizard. These are the available plan tasks:

- Back up Database Task

- Check Database Integrity Task

- Execute SQL Server Agent Job Task

- Execute T-SQL Statement Task

- History Cleanup Task

- Maintenance Cleanup Task

- Notify Operator Task

- Rebuild Index Task

- Reorganize Index Task

- Shrink Database Task

- Update Statistics Task

If you want to create a multiserver maintenance plan, the environment must have one master server and one or more target servers, and that all plans must be created and maintained only on the master server.

Data Import, Bulk Insert and BCP

You use the Import/Export Wizard to import data. It works with different data providers and even flat files.

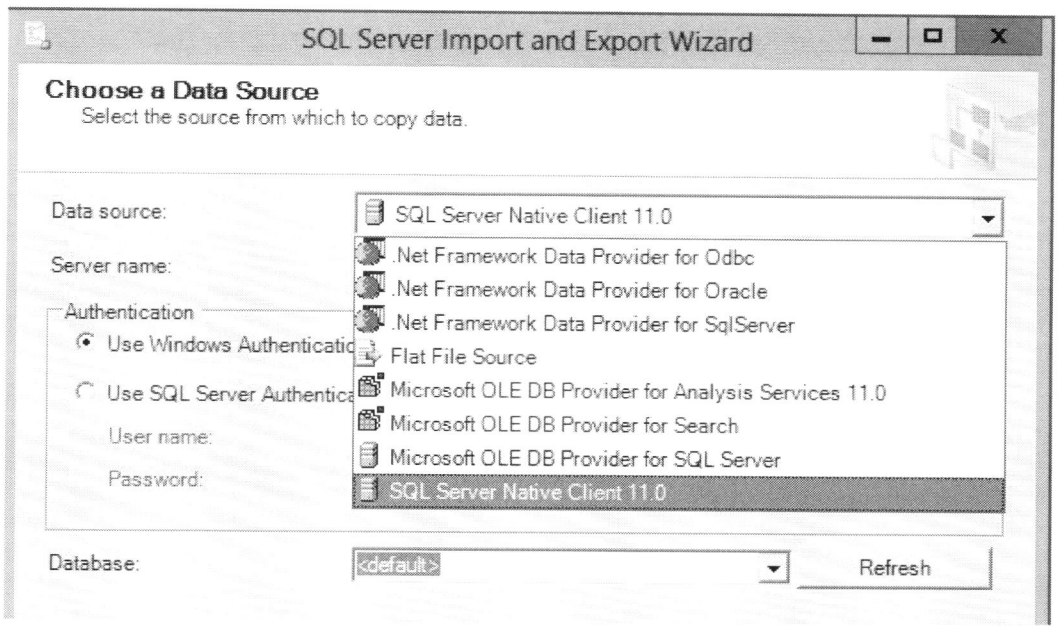

BULK INSERT can be used to import a data file into a table or view. The DATAFILETYPE value can be char (which is the default), native (database data types, which will bulk import data from SQL Server using bcp), widechar (which is Unicode), and widenative (which are native database data types except in char, varchar, and text columns). The TABLOCK option specifies that a table-level lock is used for the duration of the entire bulk-import operation. ERRORFILE can be used to specify the file that is for collecting rows that have formatting errors. Since BULK INSERT enforces strict data validation and data checks, some scripts that use it may easily fail.

The bcp utility can be used to bulk copy data between an instance and a data file in a separate user-specified format. It is intended for importing large numbers of new rows into SQL Server tables or to export data to outside data files. Without the queryout option it does not make use of T-SQL at all. To import data you need to use a format file created for your target table. You need to do so since bcp data files do not include any schema or format information. **You should use character format when bulk exporting** data to a text file or bulk importing data from a text file generated by a third party program.

Tracing and Tuning

SQL Server Profiler records events as they occur. Simply put, through a trace you can look at the commands that have been executed against the database.

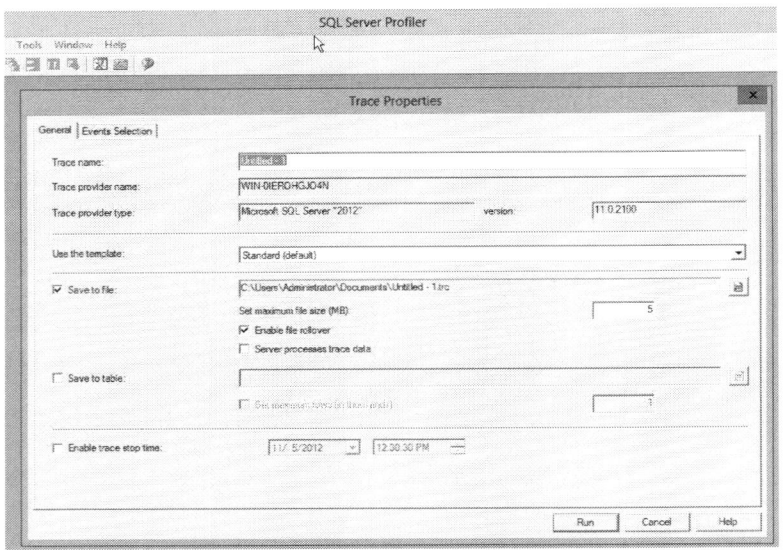

You want to know that there are different event classes. You may use the event classes in the Locks event category to monitor locking activity in an instance. The Database Event Category has event classes produced when data or log files grow or shrink. The Errors and Warnings Event Category has event classes produced when a SQL Server error or warning is raised. The Performance Event Category has event classes produced when DML operators are running. The Scans Event Category has event classes dealing with the scanning of tables and indexes. The Sessions Event Category has event classes produced when clients connect to and disconnect from an instance. The Stored Procedures Event Category has event classes dealing with the execution of stored procedures. The TSQL Event Category has event classes produced by executing T-SQL statements in an instance. The Security Audit Event Category has event classes useful for auditing server activity.

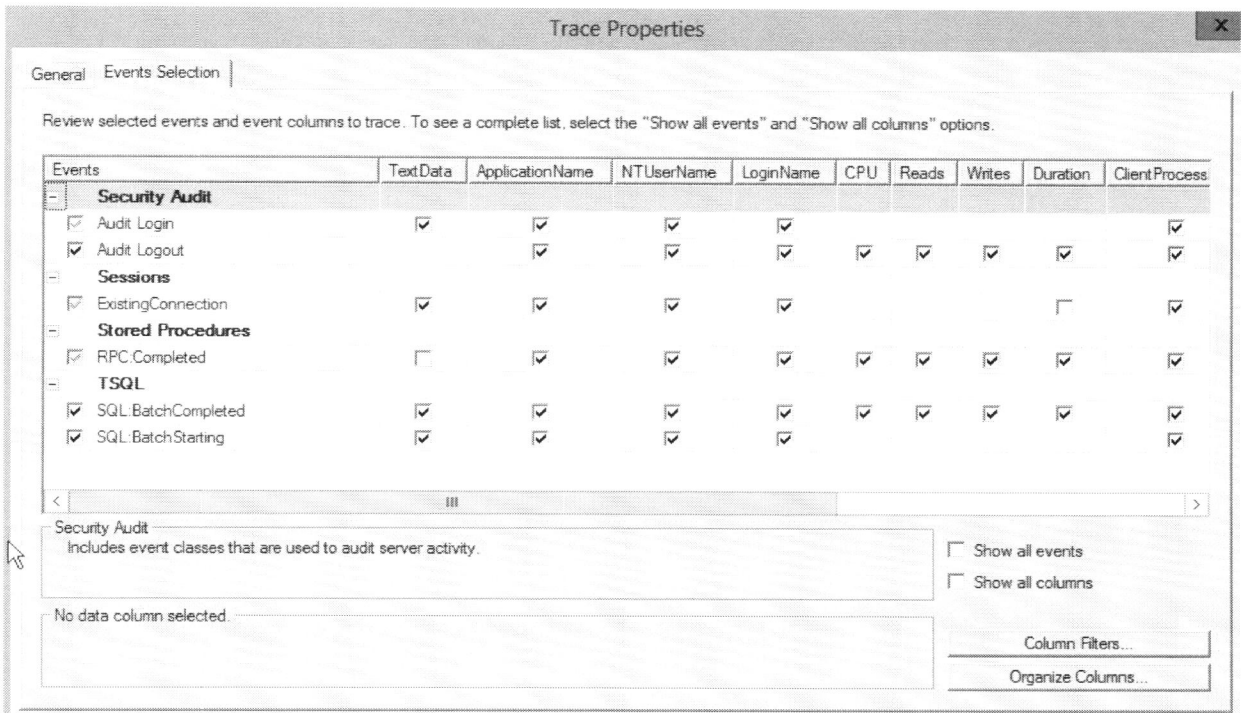

You should always save your trace to a file on the local drive. You should also click on the Events Selection tab to review the events to be monitored with your trace. Make selection or deselection accordingly. Finally, you click the Run button to start the trace.

You can base a trace on a template. The Standard template collects general information on SQL Server connections, stored procedures and T-SQL statements. The Tuning template collects information relevant for tuning

SQL Server's performance. TSQL_Replay gathers information of each T-SQL statement for recreating the same activity in the future.

You use the Database Engine Tuning Advisor to select and create an optimal set of indexes, indexed views, and partitions. Because Database Engine Tuning Advisor can and will consume system resources heavily during analysis, you should use Limit tuning time to stop tuning during periods of heavy server workload.

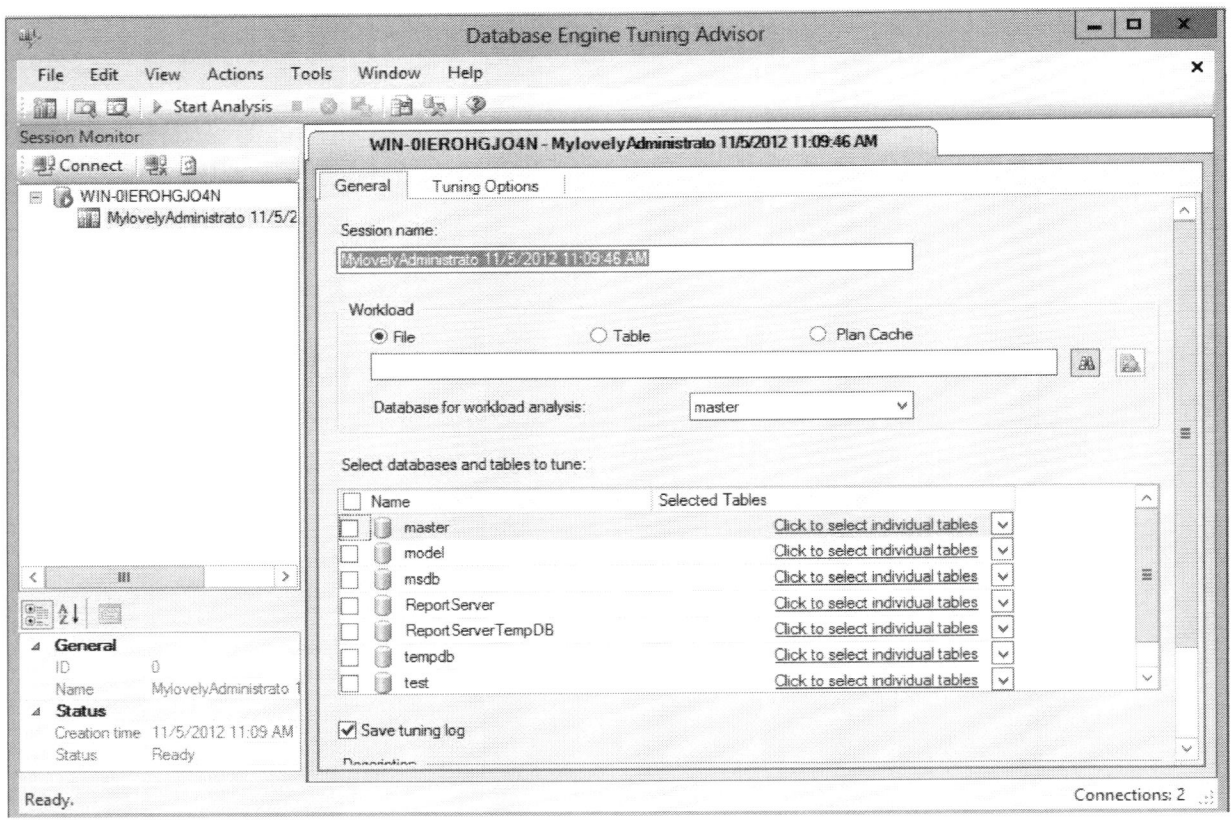

This tool analyzes workload against a physical implementation of database. The so called workload is a set of T-SQL statements that execute against a database using trace files, trace tables, and/or T-SQL scripts. When you first start it you need to specify the SQL Server instance to which you wish to connect. You need to be a member of the sysadmin fixed server role to initialize it. After this first time initialization, users that are members of the db_owner fixed database role can use it to tune those databases they own.

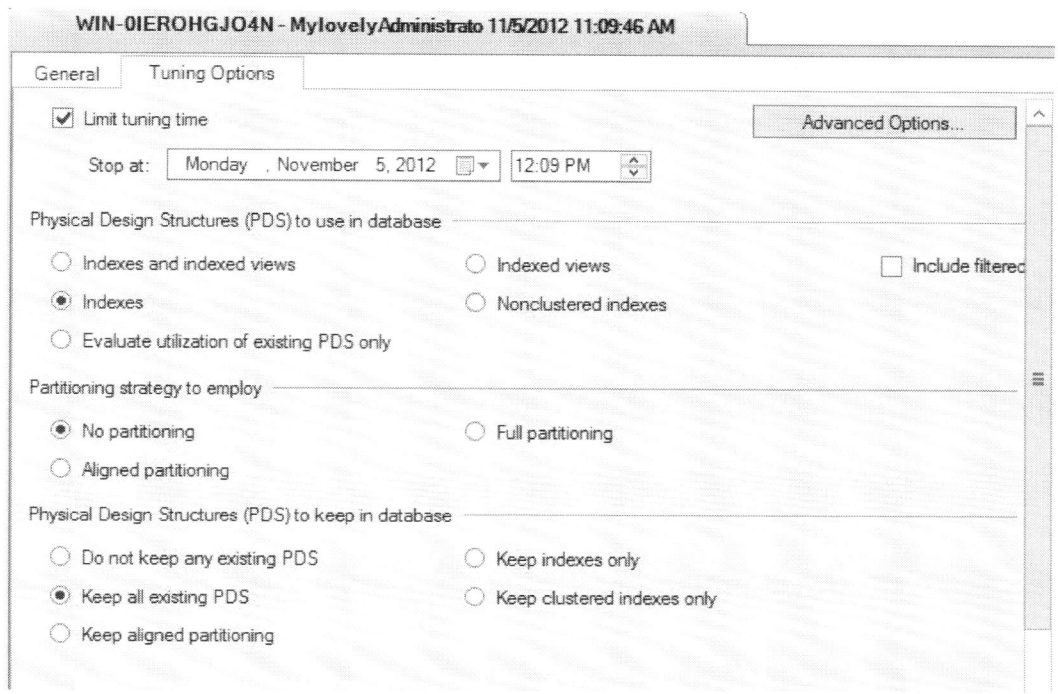

Workload analysis can be performed against these databases:

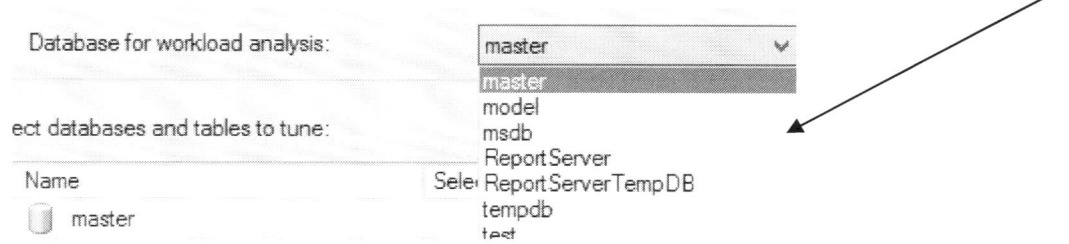

In the Advanced Options box, you can define the max space for recommendations. You can specify a maximum amount of space to be used by the physical design structures recommended by the Advisor. If no value is specified, the Advisor will assume a space limit which is 3 times the current raw data size including the total size of heaps and clustered indexes on tables in the database, OR the free space on all of the attached drives in addition to the raw data size. Also, the max columns per index field has a default of 1023.

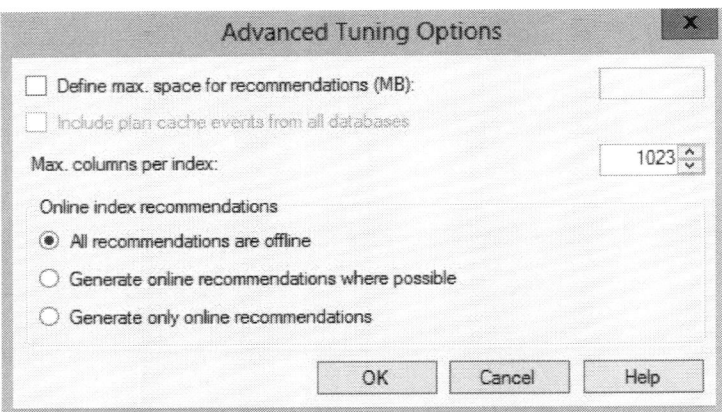

The Session Monitor shows information about sessions that are opened in the Advisor. You can also import session definitions which are in XML format.

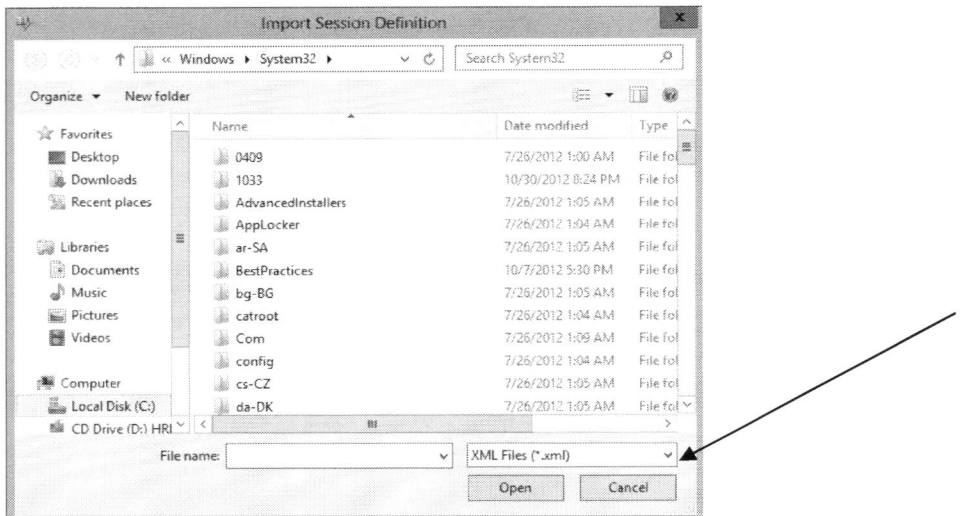

You can use the Query Editor or any text editor to create T-SQL script based workloads. Or you can create trace table workloads use SQL Server Profiler. However, if you use trace table as a workload then that table must exist on the server where Database Engine Tuning Advisor is tuning.

Constraints and Default Definitions

Constraints can be used to define how the integrity of your database can be enforced automatically. According to MS using constraints is preferred over DML Triggers, rules, and defaults.

You use NOT NULL to specify that a column does not take NULL values which implies that a value is unknown or undefined. Primary keys can enforce uniqueness but they do not allow for NULL. A FOREIGN KEY constraint can be linked to a PRIMARY KEY constraint in another table. It can also reference the columns of a UNIQUE constraint in another table.

You use a FOREIGN KEY constraint to control the data that can be stored in the foreign key table AS WELL AS to control the changes made to data in the primary key table. It enforces referential integrity through guaranteeing that one cannot make changes to data in the primary key table if those changes fail to validate the link to data in the foreign key table.

A FOREIGN KEY constraint does allow null values but verification of values that make up the FOREIGN KEY constraint will be skipped when null values are in there. When a FOREIGN KEY constraint references columns in tables in the same database or table, the table becomes a self-referencing table.

You may find the creation of an index on a foreign key useful when changes to the PRIMARY KEY constraints are checked with the FOREIGN KEY constraints in the related tables. The actual number of FOREIGN KEY constraints that one can create is in fact limited by hardware and design but you may not find it beneficial to have hundreds of such constraints in your table!

You use CHECK constraints to enforce domain integrity – that is, you want to limit the values that can be entered into a column. Technically you can use multiple CHECK constraints on a column. CHECK constraints work at the row level to reject values evaluated to FALSE. Null values often evaluate to UNKNOWN and may override a constraint. With a UNIQUE constraint, you do not allow two rows in a table to have the same value for the columns.

When loading a row into a table with a DEFAULT definition for a column, a default value will be inserted in the column whenever there is no value specified for it. You may also use DEFAULT VALUES with INSERT to explicitly insert a default value for a column. When a column does not allow for null values and there is no DEFAULT definition, you will have to explicitly specify a value in there.

Creating Indexes

You can use CREATE INDEX to create a relational index on a specified table or view. There are several important arguments you must know. UNIQUE means this is going to be a unique index. By default a clustered index on a view is always unique. Note that you cannot create a unique index on columns with duplicate values. Multiple null values are considered as duplicates! CLUSTERED means the index has a logical order of key values which determines the physical order of the corresponding rows. Each table or view can have only one clustered index at a time. A view that has a unique clustered index is an indexed view. You should ALWAYS create a clustered index prior to creating any nonclustered indexes. In fact, all the existing nonclustered indexes will get rebuilt when a clustered index is created.

When the CLUSTERED argument is not specified, a nonclustered index is the default, where the physical order of the data rows is totally independent of their indexed order. Generally, a nonclustered index can be unique or non-unique. ASC and DESC are the keywords for determining the ascending or descending sort direction for the particular index column. ASC is the default. INCLUDE can be used to specify the non-key columns to be added to the leaf level of a nonclustered index.

Columns with large object data types such as ntext, text, varchar(max), nvarchar(max), varbinary(max), xml, and image cannot be used as the key columns for an index.

A table can have max 999 nonclustered indexes either with PRIMARY KEY and UNIQUE constraints or explicitly created with CREATE INDEX. If you create a PRIMARY KEY constraint, a unique clustered index on the column will be automatically created. If you create a UNIQUE constraint, a unique nonclustered index will also be created to enforce a UNIQUE constraint.

When you have an index rebuilt or created, it is the fill-factor value that you can use to specify the percentage of space on each leaf-level page for data, and reserving the remainder as free space for accommodating future growth.

It is a percentage value from 1 to 100 while the server-wide default is 0. Page split is the process of making room for new records, which can take time and resource to perform. A proper fill value can reduce the need for page split. To change this value you need to have ALTER permission on the table or view. You can also invoke the Table Designer GUI and change this value. In any case you should be a member of the sysadmin fixed server role or the db_ddladmin and db_owner fixed database roles.

Fragmentation can exist when your indexes have pages in which the logical ordering does not match the physical ordering inside the physical file. Heavily fragmented indexes are bad for performance. You can reduce index fragmentation through rebuilding or reorganizing an index. You use the system function sys.dm_db_index_physical_stats to detect index fragmentation. The value of avg_fragmentation_in_percent describes the percentage of logical fragmentation. If the value is between 5% and 30% you should use ALTER INDEX REORGANIZE to reorganize the index. On the other hand, if the value is over 30% then you should rebuild the index entirely using ALTER INDEX REBUILD WITH (ONLINE = ON)*.

A filtered index is in fact a nonclustered index optimized with a filter predicate to index only a portion of rows in a table. This kind of index is maintained only when there are DML statements running and affecting the covered data. You need to supply the necessary SQL expression for the filtered index to be created.

XML columns are stored as binary large objects so you better give them an index. You use CREATE PRIMARY XML INDEX to produce a primary XML index which can improve XQuery performance. Or you use CREATE

XML INDEX to create secondary XML index. "Path" secondary XML index is useful for the .exist() methods. "Value" secondary XML index is for performing value-based queries when the full path is not known. "Property" secondary XML index is good when the path to the value is known.

Indexed View

In SQL Server, the result set produced by a standard view is not stored permanently. What that means is that there is an overhead of dynamically building a result set each time a query needs to reference the view. If such view is frequently referenced, you should create a unique clustered index on the view so that the result set can be stored in the database just like a table. All existing queries can benefit from the performance improvement of retrieving data from an indexed view, all without the need to rewrite any statements.

Do understand that indexed view is good mostly for views with data that is infrequently updated (such as decision support systems that are read intensive). This is due to the fact that maintenance of an indexed view can be costly. You will see performance gain on certain types of queries, such as joins and aggregations that need to process many rows, or aggregation operations that are frequently performed by a lot of queries. Queries that have very few aggregations or joins would not be suitable for indexed view. Write intensive transactions would also not be appropriate.

To create an indexed view, the ANSI_NULLS and QUOTED_IDENTIFIER options must be ON when you run CREATE VIEW using the WITH SCHEMABINDING option. The view must reference ONLY base tables in the same database as the view. Tables and user-defined functions, if any, must be referenced by two-part names. And remember, this view cannot include text, ntext, or image columns.

The first index created on this view must be a unique clustered one (you need to specify the CLUSTERED option). When you run CREATE INDEX all these must be ON: ANSI_NULLS, ANSI_PADDING, ANSI_WARNINGS, CONCAT_NULL_YIELDS_NULL, and QUOTED_IDENTIFIER.

If you disable a clustered index, the data rows of the disabled clustered index will not be accessible unless you drop or rebuild the clustered index. Operations such as SELECT, UPDATE, DELETE, INSERT, CREATE INDEX, CREATE STATISTICS, UPDATE STATISTICS and ALTER TABLE will all fail. Also, the associated nonclustered indexes will get automatically disabled and will not be enabled again until after the clustered index is re-enabled or dropped. Do note that during a SQL Server upgrade the Database Engine will automatically identify and disable an index. To disable one, use ALTER INDEX with the DISABLE option.

Aligned Index VS Nonaligned Index

An aligned index refers to an index built on the same partition scheme as its corresponding table. When a table and its indexes are aligned, SQL Server should usually be able to switch partitions more quickly and efficiently when maintaining the partition structure. For this to work the arguments of the partition functions must have the same data type, that they are defining the same number of partitions and using the same boundary values for these partitions. A nonaligned index refers to an index which is partitioned independently from its corresponding table. It is preferable when the base table is not partitioned, and that the index key is unique and without including the partitioning column of the table. You should also use it if the base table is expected to participate in collocated joins with multiple tables using multiple different join columns.

Maintaining Indexes and DBCC DBREINDEX

You can use ALTER INDEX with the REBUILD option to have an index rebuilt using the same columns, index type, uniqueness attribute, and sort order. It works just like DBCC DBREINDEX - it rebuilds a clustered index but does not rebuild the associated nonclustered indexes unless you also use the keyword ALL.

DBCC DBREINDEX allows an index to be rebuilt dynamically without the need to drop and recreate any existing PRIMARY KEY or UNIQUE constraints. If you use it to rebuild all the indexes for a table via a single statement, the operation is automatically atomic. Simply put, using DBCC DBREINDEX would be more efficient than using a bunch of individual DROP INDEX and CREATE INDEX statements. However, since DBCC DBREINDEX is an offline operation, when a nonclustered index is being rebuilt a shared lock will be held on the table which will prevent modifications to the table. When a clustered index is being rebuilt, an exclusive table lock will be held thus preventing table access entirely.

Fill Factor and Pad Index

The default for index padding is OFF. A value of ON means the percentage of free space that is specified by fill actor is to be applied to the intermediate-level pages of an index. Remember, this option is useful only when FILLFACTOR is specified. Do note that the fill factor percentage is being used only at the time of index creation. The default is 0; which has the same effect of 100, meaning SQL Server will create clustered indexes with full data pages and/or nonclustered indexes with full leaf pages, although it will leave some space within the upper level of the index tree. A small fill factor can cause SQL Server to create new indexes with pages that are not full. In other words, a small fill factor will cause each index to take relatively more storage space. This may not be bad since it allows room for data insertions without the need for the costly page splitting operation.

To avoid confusion - fill factor is the value that represents the percentage to fill the data page files on index creation at the index leaf layer. Pad Index represents the same thing at the non-leaf level. Both of them are applied when an index is created or rebuilt, therefore they are meaningless if the database is not populated.

The Execution Plan and SHOWPLAN

Index can be helpful performance-wise if you know how to create useful indexes. You need to create indexes that specifically aid the types of queries you mostly use. Generally, when you have more indexes, SELECT queries will run faster but INSERT, UPDATE, and DELETE will run slower since there are more indexes that must be maintained. There are always tradeoffs!

You should always create indexes on primary keys and foreign keys because these keys are frequently used to join tables. When you have primary key and foreign key constraints created SQL Server will automatically create indexes for them anyway.

When a query is submitted SQL Server will attempt to determine the best way to execute it via a Query Execution Plan. SQL Server can show you how it uses indexes to access or process the data for a query or other DML statements. The display of an execution plan is useful for analyzing a slow-running query. In fact, the showplan execution plan output can be generated in text or XML format. You can do so via the Management Studio GUI, by selecting Display Estimated Execution Plan or Include Actual Execution Plan from the query editor toolbar. Or, you may use these statements:

- SET SHOWPLAN_XML ON

- SET SHOWPLAN_ALL ON

- SET SHOWPLAN_TEXT ON

- SET STATISTICS XML ON

- SET STATISTICS PROFILE ON

"Display Estimated Execution Plan" is the same as using the SHOWPLAN_XML SET statement option. "Include Actual Execution Plan" is the same as using the STATISTICS XML SET statement option.

When a SET SHOWPLAN statement is ON, SQL Server will return the execution information for each statement without actually executing it. Note that you need to have sufficient permissions to execute the relevant statements and must have SHOWPLAN permission for all databases containing referenced objects. All the SET SHOWPLAN statements cannot be used inside a stored procedure since they must be the one and only one statement in a batch. SET SHOWPLAN_TEXT is for producing readable output that is to be used by Win32 command prompt applications. SET SHOWPLAN_ALL can produce more in-depth details.

SET STATISTICS XML works differently in that it allows SQL Server to execute the T-SQL statements while generating in-depth information on how the statements were executed. The document containing the output will be placed to a local directory. When SET STATISTICS PROFILE is on, each executed query will return a regular result set and then an additional result set that details the profile of the query execution. You will find it useful for ad hoc queries, views, and stored procedures.

There are also some SQL Server Profiler event classes related to showplan, which are:

- Showplan XML

- Showplan All

- Showplan Text

- Showplan XML Statistics Profile

- Showplan Statistics Profile

The SHOWPLAN permission is in fact a database-level permission which can be granted, denied, or revoked only by those with the sysadmin fixed server role, the dbcreator fixed server role (for the databases they create and own) and the db_owners fixed database role (for the databases they own). Those users who have SHOWPLAN, ALTER TRACE, or VIEW SERVER STATE permissions can all view queries captured in Showplan output, but these queries often contain sensitive information (even passwords!) so you need to be careful when granting these permissions.

Index Selectivity and sp_show_statistics

Generally you should create index on columns frequently used in the WHERE clause of your queries. Selectivity describes the ratio of qualifying rows to total rows. When the ratio is low the index is highly selective which can greatly reduce the size of the result set and thus become very useful. A unique index is supposed to have the greatest selectivity since only one row can match. You may evaluate the selectivity of an index via sp_show_statistics, which can show the current distribution statistics for a particular table and index or for all tables and indexes. When the result set indicates STALE it means the query optimizer determines that this statistic needs to be updated.

You normally want to use multiple-column indexes to evaluate filter expressions that are intended to match a prefix set of key columns. When you deploy a multiple-column index, always put the most selective columns leftmost in the key to make the index more selective.

Table Scan VS Indexing

An index scan or table scan is said to be taking place when SQL Server needs to scan the data or the index pages to find the appropriate records. A seek uses the index to pinpoint a record while a scan requires walking through every record to locate the target. Generally, proper table design and proper query optimization can avoid table scan. When you intend to store many records in a table, you should properly normalize it. If you put your queries into a store procedure, SQL Server can usually come up with an optimized execution plan for them. A table scan is much slower since every row must be scanned through. However, if you need to retrieve every row from a table for actual use then table scan is the only option anyway. Also, when your table is small or when there is very few data inside then a table scan may be simpler to use and maintain.

Index Partitioning

Partitioning a large table is recommended - by dividing the table and its indexes into smaller partitions you can maintain them on a partition-by-partition basis so to be more efficient. However, you cannot have more than 1000 partitions per table. You need to first create a partition function via CREATE PARTITION FUNCTION and specify the number of partitions, the partitioning column, and the range of partition column values for each of the partitions. Then you create a partition scheme via CREATE PARTITION SCHEME to map the partitions to a set of filegroups. Finally, you may partition a table or index at the time of creation by using CREATE TABLE or CREATE INDEX. The ON option with the partition scheme name is used to specify the partition scheme that defines the filegroups on which the partitions of a partitioned index are to be mapped.

Locking Hints

Locking is a mechanism that synchronizes access by users to the same data at the same time. When a transaction updates data, it holds a lock that protects the update until the transaction is ended. Applications seldom request locks directly as locks are managed by the lock manager.

A SQL Server database may lock data at different levels within the system hierarchy. The levels are:

- Rows

- Pages, which is a collection of rows

- Extents, which is a collection of pages

- Table

- Database

Shared locks allow concurrent transactions to SELECT a resource under pessimistic concurrency control. When there are two transactions that acquire shared-mode locks on a resource and then attempt to update the same data concurrently, one transaction will attempt to change to an exclusive lock. If both transactions are trying to convert to exclusive locks, a deadlock will occur. To avoid this sort of problem, an update lock can be used since only one transaction can obtain an update lock to a resource at any point in time. With an exclusive lock, no other transactions can change data and read operations can carry on only with the presence of a NOLOCK hint or read uncommitted isolation level. Intent locks are for signaling an intent to place locks at a lower level. They can be intent shared, intent exclusive or shared with intent exclusive.

Schema modification locks are for use during DDL operation. Schema stability locks are for use when compiling and executing queries. Bulk update locks are useful when you are bulk copying data into a table while the TABLOCK hint is there. Key-range locks are for preventing phantom reads.

SQLServer:Locks is an object that provides information about SQL Server locks on resources that prevent concurrent use by different transactions. In the context of resource monitoring, there are several resources you want to learn about. Average Wait Time tells the average amount of wait time for each lock request that resulted in a wait. Lock Timeouts (timeout > 0)/sec tells the number of lock requests per second that timed out, not including requests for NOWAIT locks.

Lock Timeouts/sec is similar and it includes those requests for NOWAIT locks. Lock Wait Time is the total wait time for locks in the last second. Number of Deadlocks/sec gives the number of lock requests per second that have resulted in deadlock.

You can override SQL Server's locking scheme by forcing locks on a table. Table-level locking hints can be used with SELECT, INSERT, UPDATE, and DELETE statements. They are:

- FASTFIRSTROW, which is suitable when a query is optimized to get the first row of the result set.

- HOLDLOCK, which is to hold a shared lock until the transaction is completed.

- NOLOCK, which is to NOT issue any shared locks or recognize exclusive locks. This should only be used with a SELECT statement.

- PAGLOCK, which is to lock the table.

- READCOMMITTED, which is to read only data from those already-committed transactions.

- READPAST, which is to have those rows locked by other processes skipped.

- READUNCOMMITTED, which is the same as NOLOCK.

- REPEATABLEREAD, which is to have locks placed on all data used in a query.

- ROWLOCK, which is to lock data at row level.

- SERIALIZABLE

- TABLOCK, which is to lock at the table level. You may want to use this when performing many operations on table-level data.

- UPDLOCK, which is to use update locks instead of shared locks when you read a table, and then hold the locks until the end of the transaction.

- XLOCK, which is to an exclusive lock on all the involved resources until the transaction is ended.

The categories for hints are granularity and isolation-level. PAGLOCK, NOLOCK, ROWLOCK, and TABLOCK are granularity hints. Examples of isolation-level hints include HOLDLOCK, NOLOCK, READCOMMITTED, REPEATABLEREAD, and SERIALIZABLE. You can use at the max one from each group at the same time. Note that it is the transaction isolation levels that define the type of locks acquired on read operations. You can use SET TRANSACTION ISOLATION LEVEL to configure it. SERIALIZABLE has the same effect as HOLDLOCK. It will make shared locks more restrictive since it will hold them until the transaction is completed. Basically, statements will not be able to read data that has been modified but not yet committed by other transactions. Also, there will be no other transactions that can modify data that has been read by the current transaction, at least not until the current transaction is completed.

The behavior of READ COMMITTED largely depends on the value of READ_COMMITTED_SNAPSHOT. If it is set to OFF (which is the default), shared locks will be used to prevent other transactions from modifying rows while the current transaction is reading, and will also block the statement from reading rows modified by other transactions, at least until the other transaction is completed. If it is set to ON, row versioning will be used to present each statement with a consistent snapshot of the data, with no lock being used to protect data from updates by other transactions. SNAPSHOT always indicates that data read by a SQL statement will be the "transactionally consistent" version of the data that existed at the beginning of the transaction, that the transaction will only recognize data modifications committed before the start of this transaction.

SQLServer:Latches is an object that provides counters for monitoring internal SQL Server resource locks. Average Latch Wait Time (ms) tells the average latch wait time for latch requests that had to wait, while Latch Waits/sec gives the number of latch requests that were not granted immediately. Total Latch Wait Time (ms) tells the total latch wait time for latch requests in the last second.

Troubleshooting Deadlocks

Locks, worker threads, memory, parallel query execution-related resources and Multiple Active Result Sets resources can all cause deadlocks. You may use SQL Server Profiler to identify the cause of a deadlock by tracing deadlock events. You do so by adding the Deadlock graph event class to a trace. This event class will populate the TextData data column of the trace with data on process and objects involved in the deadlock. This deadlock XML file which has a .xdl extension is viewable via SQL Server Management Studio. In fact both SQL Server Profiler and SQL Server Management Studio rely on a deadlock wait-for graph for describing a deadlock, by presenting process nodes, resource nodes, and edges showing the relationships between them. Both trace flag 1204 and trace flag 1222 will be generated to return information captured in the SQL Server error log. Trace flag 1204 shows deadlock information formatted by each node involved, while 1222 presents deadlock information by processes and then by resources. You may actually use both flags together to obtain two different representations of the same deadlock event.

Questions:

1. Describe the master database.

2. Describe the msdb database.

3. Describe the model database.

4. Describe the tempdb database.

5. Describe the resource database.

6. What are catalog views for?

7. When a database is upgraded to SQL Server 2012 from any earlier version, the database will retain its existing compatibility level but the minimum is:

8. When you use CREATE DATABASE, what is the option FILENAME for?

9. When you use CREATE DATABASE, what is the option UNLIMITED for?

10. You can have max _____ files and _____ filegroups for each database.

11. You can use ALTER DATABASE with the _____ option to change file sizing.

12. During bulk import, what option specifies that a table-level lock is used for the duration of the entire bulk-import operation?

13. What is the bcp utility for?

14. In terms of tracing, what is the Standard template for?

15. In terms of tracing, what is the Tuning template for?

16. In terms of tracing, what is the TSQL_Replay template for?

17. What is a filtered index?

18. Index fragmentation can exist when:

19. You can reduce index fragmentation through:

20. You can use what T-SQL statement to create a relational index on a specified table or view?

21. By default a clustered index on a view is always unique. True?

22. A SQL Server database may lock data at what levels within the system hierarchy?

23. _____ locks allow concurrent transactions to SELECT a resource under pessimistic concurrency control.

24. Schema _____ locks are for use during DDL operation. Schema _____ locks are for use when compiling and executing queries.

25. Bulk update locks are useful when you are bulk copying data into a table while the _____ hint is there.

26. Key-range locks are for preventing _____ reads.

27. _____ is an object that provides information about SQL Server locks on resources that prevent concurrent use by different transactions.

28. As a locking hint, _____ is to hold a shared lock until the transaction is completed.

29. The categories for hints are:

30. List four granularity hints.

31. Examples of isolation-level hints include (list four).

32. What defines the type of locks acquired on read operations?

33. How do you set the transaction isolation level?

34. Generally, when you have more indexes, SELECT queries will run faster but INSERT, UPDATE, and DELETE will run slower. True?

35. The default for index padding is:

36. Concerning index padding, a value of ON means:

37. What is the effect of a small fill factor?

38. Fill factor is the value that represents:

39. Fill factor and pad index are applied when:

40. How does SET STATISTICS XML work?

41. You should ALWAYS create a clustered index prior to creating any nonclustered indexes. True?

42. Physical design refers to the process of producing:

43. ER Modeling involves developing a visual representation of the real world problem as:

44. Describe logical database design.

45. What does high data cardinality imply?

46. Constraints can be used to define:

47. You use a FOREIGN KEY constraint to control:

48. You use _____ constraints to enforce domain integrity and limit the values that can be entered into a column.

49. What is the benefit of using an aligned index?

50. What T-SQL statement works just like DBCC DBREINDEX?

51. Indexed view is good mostly for views with data that is infrequently updated. True?

52. To create an indexed view, the ANSI_NULLS and QUOTED_IDENTIFIER options must be _____ when you run CREATE VIEW using the WITH SCHEMABINDING option.

53. Compare the scope of local temporary tables and global temporary tables.

54. The name specified for a temporary name should not exceed ____ characters.

55. What can cause deadlocks?

56. How do you use SQL Server Profiler to identify the cause of a deadlock?

57. Describe 1NF.

58. Describe 3NF and 4NF.

59. What is a contained database?

60. An existing database can be converted to a partially contained database by using ALTER DATABASE with:

Answers:

1. *The master database is for recording system-level information for an instance.*

2. *The msdb database is for used by the SQL Server Agent to schedule alerts and jobs.*

3. *The model database is the template for all databases created on the instance.*

4. The *tempdb database is simply a workspace for holding temporary objects and result sets.*

5. The *resource database is read-only and is for holding system objects that are included with SQL Server.*

6. *Catalog views are designed for returning information used by the SQL Server Database Engine.*

7. *When a database is upgraded to SQL Server 2012 from any earlier version, the database will retain its existing compatibility level but the minimum is 90.*

8. FILENAME *lets you specify the physical filename.*

9. UNLIMITED *means the file can grow until the disk is full.*

10. *You can have max 32,767 files and 32,767 filegroups for each database.*

11. *You can use ALTER DATABASE with the MODIFY FILE option to change file sizing.*

12. *The TABLOCK option specifies that a table-level lock is used for the duration of the entire bulk-import operation.*

13. *The bcp utility can be used to bulk copy data between an instance and a data file in a separate user-specified format. It is intended for importing large numbers of new rows into SQL Server tables or to export data to outside data files.*

14. *The Standard template collects general information on SQL Server connections, stored procedures and T-SQL statements.*

15. *The Tuning template collects information relevant for tuning SQL Server's performance.*

16. TSQL_Replay *gathers information of each T-SQL statement for recreating the same activity in the future.*

17. *A filtered index is in fact a nonclustered index optimized with a filter predicate to index only a portion of rows in a table. This kind of index is maintained only when there are DML statements running and affecting the covered data.*

18. *Fragmentation can exist when your indexes have pages in which the logical ordering does not match the physical ordering inside the physical file. Heavily fragmented indexes are bad for performance.*

19. *You can reduce index fragmentation through rebuilding or reorganizing an index.*

20. *You can use CREATE INDEX to create a relational index on a specified table or view.*

21. *By default a clustered index on a view is always unique.*

22. *A SQL Server database may lock data at different levels within the system hierarchy. The levels are: Rows, Pages, Extents, Table and Database.*

23. *Shared locks allow concurrent transactions to SELECT a resource under pessimistic concurrency control.*

24. *Schema modification locks are for use during DDL operation. Schema stability locks are for use when compiling and executing queries.*

25. *Bulk update locks are useful when you are bulk copying data into a table while the TABLOCK hint is there.*

26. *Key-range locks are for preventing phantom reads.*

27. *SQLServer:Locks is an object that provides information about SQL Server locks on resources that prevent concurrent use by different transactions.*

28. *As a locking hint, HOLDLOCK is to hold a shared lock until the transaction is completed.*

29. *The categories for hints are granularity and isolation-level.*

30. PAGLOCK, NOLOCK, ROWLOCK, and TABLOCK are granularity hints.

31. Examples of isolation-level hints include HOLDLOCK, NOLOCK, READCOMMITTED, REPEATABLEREAD, and SERIALIZABLE.

32. It is the transaction isolation levels that define the type of locks acquired on read operations.

33. You can use SET TRANSACTION ISOLATION LEVEL to configure it.

34. Generally, when you have more indexes, SELECT queries will run faster but INSERT, UPDATE, and DELETE will run slower.

35. The default for index padding is OFF.

36. A value of ON means the percentage of free space that is specified by fill actor is to be applied to the intermediate-level pages of an index.

37. A small fill factor can cause SQL Server to create new indexes with pages that are not full.

38. Fill factor is the value that represents the percentage to fill the data page files on index creation at the index leaf layer. Pad Index represents the same thing at the non-leaf level.

39. Both of them are applied when an index is created or rebuilt, therefore they are meaningless if the database is not populated.

40. SET STATISTICS XML allows SQL Server to execute the T-SQL statements while generating in-depth information on how the statements were executed.

41. You should ALWAYS create a clustered index prior to creating any nonclustered indexes.

42. Physical design refers to the process of producing a detailed database specific data model to meet end user requirements.

43. *ER Modeling involves developing a visual representation of the real world problem as an ERD Entity Relationship Diagram and have the details modeled in terms of entities, attributes and relations.*

44. *Logical database design which is not specific to the database requires the construction of a model of information that can be mapped into the various SQL Server database objects.*

45. *Data cardinality refers to the uniqueness of data values contained in a column. With high data cardinality the values of a data column are very uncommon, that uniqueness is more likely.*

46. *Constraints can be used to define the way the integrity of a database is enforced automatically.*

47. *You use a FOREIGN KEY constraint to control the data that can be stored in the foreign key table AS WELL AS to control the changes made to data in the primary key table.*

48. *You use CHECK constraints to enforce domain integrity and limit the values that can be entered into a column.*

49. *An aligned index refers to an index built on the same partition scheme as its corresponding table. When a table and its indexes are aligned, SQL Server should usually be able to switch partitions more quickly and efficiently when maintaining the partition structure.*

50. *You can use ALTER INDEX with the REBUILD option to have an index rebuilt using the same columns, index type, uniqueness attribute, and sort order. It works just like DBCC DBREINDEX.*

51. *Do understand that indexed view is good mostly for views with data that is infrequently updated (such as decision support systems that are read intensive).*

52. To create an indexed view, the *ANSI_NULLS* and *QUOTED_IDENTIFIER* options must be ON when you run CREATE VIEW using the WITH SCHEMABINDING option.

53. Local temporary tables are visible in the current session, while global temporary tables are visible to all the active sessions.

54. The name specified for a temporary name should not exceed 116 characters.

55. Locks, worker threads, memory, parallel query execution-related resources and Multiple Active Result Sets resources can all cause deadlocks.

56. You may use SQL Server Profiler to identify the cause of a deadlock by tracing deadlock events. You do so by adding the Deadlock graph event class to a trace.

57. First normal form 1NF requires that you eliminate duplicative columns from the same table and create separate tables for each group of related data. You also need to identify each row with a unique column or a unique set of columns to serve as the primary key.

58. Third Normal Form 3NF further requires that you remove all those columns that are not dependent on the primary key. Fourth Normal Form 4NF further requires that all multi-valued dependencies be removed.

59. A contained database refers to a database isolated from other databases and also from the instance of SQL Server that hosts this database.

60. An existing database can be converted to a partially contained database by using ALTER DATABASE with SET CONTAINMENT = PARTIAL.

SQL Statements

T-SQL Statements

You use Data definition language DDL to create and delete databases/tables, define table rows and columns, create indexes, and take other actions that change the structure of the database. On the other hand, you use Data manipulation language DML to run queries and add, delete, or edit records. From a pure performance perspective, implementing SQL using Stored Procedures can eliminate any duplicate SQLs and improve performance since stored procedures tend to run faster on the server.

SELECT and the possible options

You need to have SELECT permission on the table or view. This permission may in fact be inherited from the SELECT permission on the schema or CONTROL permission on the table. Member of the db_datareader/db_owner fixed database roles or the sysadmin fixed server role can always run SELECT at wish. You want to know that there is a logical processing order for a SELECT statement, which is:

- FROM

- ON

- JOIN

- WHERE

- GROUP BY

- WITH CUBE or WITH ROLLUP

- HAVING

- DISTINCT

- ORDER BY

- TOP

With the DISTINCT argument, only unique rows can appear in the result set, which is NOT the default. With TOP, only a specified first set or percent of rows can be returned. SELECT…INTO can be used to create a new table in the default filegroup with the insertion of the resulting rows from the query into it. The format of the new table is primarily determined by the expressions supplied in the select list, and that you simply cannot use it to create a partitioned table even when the source table itself is a partitioned one.

A subquery is an inner select, which is always enclosed in parentheses. It cannot have any COMPUTE or FOR BROWSE clause. However, it can have an ORDER BY clause when a TOP clause is also in there. Generally you can have a subquery nested inside the WHERE or HAVING clause of an outer SELECT, INSERT, UPDATE, or DELETE statement. You can even allow the subquery to stay inside another subquery, with max 32 levels of nesting possible. Do note that when a table appears only in a subquery but not in the outer query, the columns from that table will not be available in the output.

COMPUTE and the possible options

COMPUTE can be used to generate subtotals in a result set. You can actually specify COMPUTE BY and COMPUTE in the same query. The row aggregate functions that are commonly used with COMPUTE include:

- AVG, which compute the average of all values in a numeric expression.

- COUNT, which gives the exact number of selected rows.

- MAX, which gives the highest value in an expression.

- MIN, which gives the lowest value in an expression.

- SUM, which produces the total of all values in a numeric expression.

You should not use the COUNT() aggregate in a subquery for performing an existence check since it will count all matching values via a table scan or a scan of the smallest non-clustered index, which is not too efficient (in fact, using COUNT(*) to obtain record count in a table can be slow due to the possibly of a table scan.). You should use EXISTS instead. Do note that ntext, text, and image cannot be dealt with through COMPUTE or COMPUTE BY.

FOR and the possible options

You use FOR to specify either the BROWSE or the XML option. You use BROWSE to specify that updates be allowed when you view data under a

DB-Library browse mode cursor, which allows you to scan rows in a table and update data one row at a time. There is one major limitation - FOR BROWSE cannot be used in SELECT statements joined by the UNION operator. You can actually turn on the NO_BROWSETABLE option via SET NO_BROWSETABLE ON so that all the SELECT statements will behave as if the FOR BROWSE option has been appended to the statements. If you use the XML argument, the results of the query will be returned as an XML document. The possible modes are RAW, AUTO, and EXPLICIT. The RAW mode generates a single <row> element per row in the returned rowset. The AUTO mode supports nesting in the resulting XML. The EXPLICIT mode gives you more control over how the XML results are formatted.

GROUP BY, HAVING and the possible options

You use GROUP BY to group a selected set of rows into a set of summary rows by the values of columns or expressions, while only one row will get returned for each group. Although there are both an ISO-compliant syntax and a non-ISO-compliant syntax, you should use the former unless backward compatibility is necessary. The ROLLUP ( ) argument can be used to generate the simple GROUP BY aggregate rows as well as the subtotal/super-aggregate rows and also a grand total row. The GROUPING SETS ( ) argument can be used to specify multiple groupings of data in a single query.

You use HAVING for specifying search condition for a group or an aggregate. You can use HAVING only with a SELECT statement. You may want to use it inside a GROUP BY clause. However, text, image, and ntext cannot be used in the HAVING clause.

ORDER BY and the possible options

You use ORDER BY to order the result set of a query and at the same time limit the rows that are returned. You use COLLATE to specify that operation should be performed following a different collation. You use OFFSET to specify the number of rows to be skipped. You can further use FETCH to specify the number of rows to return as soon as the OFFSET clause is processed. MS recommends that whenever you use the SELECT TOP statement you use the ORDER BY clause to predictably indicate the rows that are to be affected by the TOP option.

OVER and the possible options

OVER can be used to determine the partitioning and ordering of a rowset before allowing the associated window function to be applied - you use it to define a window or custom set of rows within a query result set. With the PARTITION BY argument the window function will be applied to each partition separately and that computation will be restarted for each partition. UNBOUNDED PRECEDING means the window will start at the first row of the partition. You can use multiple window functions in a single query, and that the OVER clause deployed for each function can actually differ both in partitioning and in ordering.

Ranking, Aggregate, Analytic and Date/Time Functions

You use ranking functions to return a ranking value for each row within a partition. They are nondeterministic. Examples include:

- RANK

- NTILE

- DENSE_RANK

- ROW_NUMBER

You use aggregate functions to calculate on a set of values in order to return a single value. Simply put, they generate summary values in query result sets. All of these functions other than COUNT will ignore null value by default. In fact they are frequently used with GROUP BY. By the way, all of them are deterministic! Also, NULL values are always excluded in aggregate results.

Examples of aggregate functions include:

- AVG

- MIN

- CHECKSUM_AGG

- SUM

- COUNT

- STDEV

- COUNT_BIG

- STDEVP

- GROUPING

- VAR

- GROUPING_ID

- VARP

- MAX

You use analytic functions to compute an aggregate value based on a group of rows, that it is possible for them to return more than one row for each group. You may want to use them to compute things like moving averages, running totals, percentages ...etc. Examples include:

- CUME_DIST

- LEAD

- FIRST_VALUE

- PERCENTILE_CONT

- LAG

- PERCENTILE_DISC

- LAST_VALUE

- PERCENT_RANK

You use the GETDATE function to retrieve the current date and time in SQL Server. You use the DATEADD function to produce a new date/time value which is based on adding an interval to the concerned date. You use the DATEDIFF function to produce the number of date/time boundaries that get crossed between two different dates. You use DATEPART to produce an integer that forms a specified part of a date.

Truncate Table

You can use TRUNCATE TABLE to delete all rows from a table without logging the individual row deletions. Although functionally it is the same as running the DELETE statement with no WHERE clause, it is faster and it uses fewer resources since fewer locks will be used. By default, the TRUNCATE TABLE permissions are granted to the table owner, the members of the sysadmin fixed server role and the db_owner/db_ddladmin fixed database roles. Note that you cannot run TRUNCATE TABLE on tables that are referenced by a FOREIGN KEY constraint UNLESS the foreign key is referencing itself. You also cannot run TRUNCATE TABLE on tables that participate in an indexed view. Also note that TRUNCATE TABLE cannot fire any trigger since individual row deletions are never logged.

Triggers

You use CREATE TRIGGER to create a trigger, which is in fact a special kind of stored procedure that will automatically run when an event takes place. If CREATE TRIGGER is part of a batch, it must be the first statement. CREATE TRIGGER can apply to only one table in the current database even though it can reference objects in another database.

DML triggers are invoked when a user modifies data through DML. DDL triggers get invoked due to DDL events. Logon triggers are special in that they fire primarily in response to the LOGON event, which is raised only when a user session is getting established.

There are some important arguments you want to know. DATABASE means the DDL trigger is for applying to the entire database. ALL SERVER means the DDL/logon trigger is to be applied to the current server. WITH ENCRYPTION can be used to prevent the trigger from being published during replication. EXECUTE AS is for explicitly specifying the security context under which the current trigger fires.

You use AFTER to specify that the DML trigger can be fired only when all operations in the triggering SQL statement are successfully completed. All referential cascade actions and constraint checks also must succeed before this trigger fires. It is in fact the default when FOR is also there.

You use INSTEAD OF to specify that the DML trigger is to be executed instead of the triggering statement. You cannot use INSTEAD OF for DDL or logon triggers. Also, you can have only one INSTEAD OF trigger per INSERT, UPDATE, or DELETE statement on a table or view.

By default triggers can be nested up to max 32 levels. You may disable nested triggers by setting the nested triggers option of sp_configure to a value of 0. You may create a DML trigger if you have ALTER permission on the table or view on which the trigger is to be created. You may create a DDL trigger with server scope or a logon trigger if you have CONTROL SERVER permission on the server. Or you may create a DDL trigger with database scope if you have ALTER ANY DATABASE DDL TRIGGER permission in the current database.

Joins

You use joins to retrieve data from two or more tables or views. With an inner join, the records from two sources will be combined and added to a query's results when the values of the joined fields can meet the criteria you define. An outer join is different in that it will return all rows from the joined tables or views even when there is no matching row between them. There are in fact three types of outer joins, which are left, right, and full, that indicate the main data's source. You can have inner joins specified in the FROM clause or the WHERE clauses. Outer joins, in contrast, can be specified only in the FROM clause.

When you use a left outer join to combine rows from two sources, all the rows from the left side will be included. A right outer join is the exact opposite. A full outer join will simply retrieve all the rows from both sides, that all of the paired rows where the join condition is evaluated to true will be retrieved. This type of join is less popular. A cross join is special in that it will return the product but not the sum of two sources - we are talking about the set of all possible row combinations without filtering here. A self join means a table or view is joined to itself, which is a form of reflexive relationship.

You cannot have tables joined directly basing on ntext, text, or image columns. However, this can be done indirectly using SUBSTRING. Generally, columns involved in a join condition need not be of the same data type, but they must be at least compatible or convertible. Sometimes you may need to explicitly convert the data through using the CAST function.

You should avoid including unnecessary columns in the SELECT list. You should also avoid unnecessary tables in your join conditions. Joining LOB columns can be very costly. And, when joining two columns of different types, conversion will take place which can slow things down. Joining tables with incompatible types can be particularly slow!

The UNION operator

UNION can be used to combine the results of multiple queries into a single result set which includes all the rows that belong to all queries participated in the union. Technically it is different from using joins to combine columns from tables. Without ALL, duplicates are excluded. You want to know that it is more efficient then using OR in a query. UNION ALL is even faster since it does need to worry about duplicates removal.

CREATE VIEW and the possible options

When you use CREATE VIEW to create a view, there are some important arguments you need to know. You use WITH CHECK OPTION to force those data modification statements executed against the view to strictly follow the criteria specified within the SELECT statement. When a row is being modified through the view, WITH CHECK OPTION can be used to ensure that the data will remain visible through the view. SCHEMABINDING can be used to ensure that the base table cannot be modified to affect the view definition.

Note that you can create new view only in the current database, and that CREATE VIEW must be the first statement in the query. You can give the new view max 1024 columns. When a view depends on a table or another view that has been dropped, you will get an error. HOWEVER, when a new table or view is created and the table structure is the same, the view can be used again. If the base table or view has a structural change, the view will have to be dropped and recreated from scratch again.

It is technically possible to modify the data of an underlying base table through a view if the columns to be modified in the view are directly referencing the underlying data in the table columns, and that the columns are not derived from any aggregate function or computation. The UPDATE, INSERT, or DELETE statements you use must reference columns from only a single base table.

SEQUENCE

Technically, a sequence is a user-defined schema bound object for generating a sequence of numeric values. It is not tied to any table. The values to be generated may include:

- tinyint, from 0 to 255

- smallint, from -32,768 to 32,767

- int, from -2,147,483,648 to 2,147,483,647

- bigint, from -9,223,372,036,854,775,808 to 9,223,372,036,854,775,807. It is the default.

You use CREATE SEQUENCE to create a sequence. By default, those with the db_owner and db_ddladmin fixed database roles may create, alter, and drop sequence objects. Those with the db_owner and db_datawriter fixed database roles may also update sequence objects and cause them to generate numbers. The START WITH option can be used to specify a value less than or equal to the maximum and greater than or equal to the minimum value specified for the sequence object. INCREMENT BY can be used to specify a value to increment or decrement the sequence object. When the increment is negative then the sequence object is descending. MINVALUE and MAXVALUE are for specifying the bounds for the sequence object. CYCLE | NO CYCLE tells if the sequence object should restart from the minimum value when generating numbers. The default is NO CYCLE, which means an exception will result when the max value is exceeded.

Full-Text Search

You may issue full-text queries against character-based data in a table when there is a full-text index on that table. This full-text index includes character-based columns which can have data types such as char, varchar, nchar, nvarchar, text, ntext, image, xml, and varbinary. For each supported language there is also a language-specific linguistic component.

Full-text predicates that can be used include CONTAINS and FREETEXT. You can have CONTAINS and FREETEXT specified in the WHERE or HAVING clause. Through them you may specify the selection criteria for determining whether a row would match the full-text query. Generally, you should use CONTAINS for precise or fuzzy matches. You may also use logical operation between multiple search conditions. Or, you may use FREETEXT to match the meaning (not wording) of words, phrases and freetext strings.

The supported rowset-valued functions for full text query include CONTAINSTABLE and FREETEXTTABLE. Both of them can be referenced like a table in the FROM clause of a SELECT statement. The result to be returned may be a table of zero, one, or multiple rows that match the full-text query.

The LIKE operator can be used in a regular SELECT statement with a WHERE clause. You do this to search for a specified pattern in a column. Note that a LIKE search is believed to be less efficient and less sophisticated than a full text search.

Explicit Transaction

Transaction is defined by MS as a sequence of operations performed as a single logical unit of work. Atomic means that every piece of work in the transaction is an integral part of a single unit, that ALL works within the transaction must complete for the transaction to be considered as committed. A completed transaction should leave the database in a consistent internal state and should provide a consistent view of the data while being permanently stored in the system.

You want to know that Windows Server has a Distributed Transaction Coordinator DTC service that can coordinate transactions that update multiple transaction protected resources (including databases) on a single server computer or distributed across networked server computers. Mutual Authentication Required is the highest secured communication mode you can use in a non-clustered setup.

If you need to perform multi statement transactions, you need to have a BEGIN TRAN at the beginning and a COMMIT TRAN at the end. Everything in between these statements is considered a logical unit of work. To roll back a transaction, use ROLLBACK TRAN which can undo all the work since the last BEGIN TRAN statement.

Catching errors in statements

Errors in your T-SQL codes can be processed by the TRY…CATCH block. When an error is detected inside a TRY block, control will be passed to a

CATCH block where the error can be dealt with. After the CATCH block takes care of the problem, control will be transferred to the first statement that follows END CATCH. You can also use RAISERROR in either the TRY or CATCH block to fine tune error-handling. With a severity of 11 to 19 inside a TRY block control will be transferred to the associated CATCH block. RAISERROR can provide information to the caller on the error that caused the CATCH block to run. Note that RAISERROR with a severity 10 or lower will only return an informational message to the calling batch without invoking CATCH. On the other hand, RAISERROR with a severity 20 or higher will directly close the database connection without invoking CATCH. An alternative is the THROW statement, which can raise an exception and transfer execution to CATCH within a TRY…CATCH block. In fact, any error that takes place in a THROW statement will cause a statement batch to end. The link listed below provides a table of error severities:

http://msdn.microsoft.com/en-us/library/ms164086.aspx

Questions:

1. With the _____ argument, only unique rows can appear in the result set produced by SELECT.

2. With _____, only a specified first set or percent of rows can be returned by SELECT.

3. You may use what kind of functions to compute an aggregate value based on a group of rows?

4. _____ can be used to determine the partitioning and ordering of a rowset before allowing the associated window function to be applied.

5. You use _____ to group a selected set of rows into a set of summary rows by the values of columns or expressions.

6. You use _____ to specify either the BROWSE or the XML option.

7. You use HAVING for specifying:

8. You can use HAVING only with a SELECT statement. True?

9. NULL values are not included in aggregate results. True?

10. You use the _____ function to retrieve the current date and time in SQL Server.

11. You use the _____ function to produce a new date/time value which is based on adding an interval to the concerned date.

12. Describe a left join.

13. What does a full outer join do?

14. What can be produced by a cross join?

15. Compare DDL with DML.

16. You can have inner joins specified in the FROM clause or the _____ clauses.

17. You can allow a subquery to stay inside another subquery, with max _____ levels of nesting possible.

18. When a table appears only in a subquery but not in the outer query, the columns from that table will not be available in the output. True?

19. _____ can be used to generate subtotals in a result set.

20. By default triggers can be nested up to max ___ levels.

21. You may disable nested triggers by setting the nested triggers option of _____ to a value of 0.

22. You may create a DML trigger if you have _____ permission on the table or view on which the trigger is to be created.

23. You may create a DDL trigger with server scope or a logon trigger if you have _____ permission on the server.

24. By default, the TRUNCATE TABLE permissions are granted to:

25. You cannot run TRUNCATE TABLE on tables that are referenced by a FOREIGN KEY constraint UNLESS:

26. It is technically possible to modify the data of an underlying base table through a view. True?

27. You can give a view max _____ columns.

28. Full-text predicates that can be used include CONTAINS and:

29. Generally, you should use _____ for precise or fuzzy matches.

30. The supported rowset-valued functions for full text query include:

31. The _____ operator can be used in a regular SELECT statement with a WHERE clause. You do this to search for a specified pattern in a column.

32. _____ can be used to combine the results of multiple queries into a single result set which includes all the rows that belong to all queries participated in the union.

33. UNION ALL is faster than UNION due to what reason?

34. When a table appears only in a subquery but not in the outer query, the columns from that table will not be available in the output. True?

35. If you need to perform multi statement transactions, you need to have a BEGIN TRAN at the beginning and a _____ at the end.

36. You use _____ to create a sequence.

37. The _____ option can be used to specify a value less than or equal to the maximum and greater than or equal to the minimum value specified for the sequence object.

38. _____ can be used to specify a value to increment or decrement the sequence object.

Answers:

1. *With the DISTINCT argument, only unique rows can appear in the result set, which is NOT the default.*

2. *With TOP, only a specified first set or percent of rows can be returned.*

3. *You use analytic functions to compute an aggregate value based on a group of rows, that it is possible for them to return more than one row for each group.*

4. *OVER can be used to determine the partitioning and ordering of a rowset before allowing the associated window function to be applied.*

5. *You use GROUP BY to group a selected set of rows into a set of summary rows by the values of columns or expressions, while only one row will get returned for each group.*

6. *You use FOR to specify either the BROWSE or the XML option.*

7. *You use HAVING for specifying search condition for a group or an aggregate.*

8. *You can use HAVING only with a SELECT statement.*

9. *NULL values are not included in aggregate results.*

10. *You use the GETDATE function to retrieve the current date and time in SQL Server.*

11. *You use the DATEADD function to produce a new date/time value which is based on adding an interval to the concerned date.*

12. *When you use a left outer join to combine two sources, all the rows from the left side will be included. A right outer join is the exact opposite.*

13. *A full outer join will simply retrieve all the rows from both sides, that all of the paired rows where the join condition is evaluated to true will be retrieved. This type of join is less popular.*

14. *A cross join is special in that it will return the product but not the sum of two sources - we are talking about the set of all possible row combinations without filtering here.*

15. *You use Data definition language DDL to create and delete databases/tables, define table rows and columns, create indexes, and take other actions that change the structure of the database. On the other hand, you use Data manipulation language DML to run queries and add, delete, or edit records.*

16. *You can have inner joins specified in the FROM clause or the WHERE clauses. Outer joins, in contrast, can be specified only in the FROM clause.*

17. *A subquery is an inner select, which is always enclosed in parentheses.*

18. *You can allow the subquery to stay inside another subquery, with max 32 levels of nesting possible.*

19. *COMPUTE can be used to generate subtotals in a result set.*

20. *By default triggers can be nested up to max 32 levels.*

21. *You may disable nested triggers by setting the nested triggers option of sp_configure to a value of 0.*

22. You may create a DML trigger if you have ALTER permission on the table or view on which the trigger is to be created.

23. You may create a DDL trigger with server scope or a logon trigger if you have CONTROL SERVER permission on the server.

24. By default, the TRUNCATE TABLE permissions are granted to the table owner, the members of the sysadmin fixed server role and the db_owner/db_ddladmin fixed database roles.

25. You cannot run TRUNCATE TABLE on tables that are referenced by a FOREIGN KEY constraint UNLESS the foreign key is referencing itself.

26. It is technically possible to modify the data of an underlying base table through a view if the columns to be modified in the view are directly referencing the underlying data in the table columns, and that the columns are not derived from any aggregate function or computation.

27. You can give a view max 1024 columns.

28. Full-text predicates that can be used include CONTAINS and FREETEXT.

29. Generally, you should use CONTAINS for precise or fuzzy matches.

30. The supported rowset-valued functions for full text query include CONTAINSTABLE and FREETEXTTABLE.

31. The LIKE operator can be used in a regular SELECT statement with a WHERE clause. You do this to search for a specified pattern in a column.

32. UNION can be used to combine the results of multiple queries into a single result set which includes all the rows that belong to all queries participated in the union.

33. UNION ALL is faster since it does need to worry about duplicates removal.

34. *When a table appears only in a subquery but not in the outer query, the columns from that table will not be available in the output.*

35. *If you need to perform multi statement transactions, you need to have a BEGIN TRAN at the beginning and a COMMIT TRAN at the end.*

36. *You use CREATE SEQUENCE to create a sequence.*

37. *The START WITH option can be used to specify a value less than or equal to the maximum and greater than or equal to the minimum value specified for the sequence object.*

38. *INCREMENT BY can be used to specify a value to increment or decrement the sequence object.*

End of book

Printed in Great Britain
by Amazon